HE SAID...SHE SAID

Bernard Share

He Said...She Said

Quotes of
the Year
2010

Gill & Macmillan

Gill & Macmillan Ltd
Hume Avenue, Park West, Dublin 12
with associated companies throughout the world
www.gillmacmillan.ie

© Selection Bernard Share 2010
978 07171 4793 9

Index compiled by Helen Litton
Typography design by Bill Bolger
Print origination by Carole Lynch
Printed and bound in the UK by CPI Mackays, Chatham ME5 8TD

This book is typeset in Quadraat Regular 9.5pt on 12pt.

The paper used in this book comes from the
wood pulp of managed forests. For every tree
felled, at least one tree is planted, thereby
renewing natural resources.

A CIP catalogue record for this book is available
from the British Library.

1 3 5 4 2

Contents

Foreword

A year of crux and crisis: floods, snow, ash, NAMA, Anglo, Lisbon and Thierry Henry: but the big events do not always produce the telling phrases—the media obsessively warn of 'chaos'; politicians become over-devoted to 'going forward'; clichés and tired old locutions tumble out, too many eggs in one basket. There are of course, the exceptions, the best of which, I hope, have been accorded due recognition in these pages. Happily, however, those who wield power and self-assumed authority often find themselves upstaged by ordinary people (even very ordinary people: see Ahern, Bertie), the Joe and Josephine Soaps who can fashion the memorable utterance even when up to their eyeballs in floodwater or debt.

The collection is drawn from this island north, south, east and west as well as from those foreign fields historically, practically, temperamentally or temporarily infected by Irishness. The overriding criterion, however, remains as the poet Alexander Pope stated it a few centuries since: 'What oft was thought, but ne'er so well expressed.'

Bishops, barmen, fashionistas, farmerettes—what they all have to say is here set down as it was reported, torts and all, only obvious typos and eccentric punctuation being silently amended. And those of a sensitive nature should be advised that this is a ****-free zone.

I must record my grateful thanks to Bill Bolger, Allen Foster and Jonathan Williams for advice, professional assistance and encouragement, but the overall responsibility for the selection of what follows remains, of course, my own.

Bernard Share,
October 2010

Right now, we're planning to buy a dog

—says Siobhán Greaney: 'a retriever, whom we plan to name Millie'. She and her husband, Noel, from Carnmore, Oranmore, Co. Galway, have chosen the name in honour of their €9.8 million euro-jackpot win. 'After that', she adds, 'it will be back to normal, we hope.'

As the campaign reaches its climax, the re-run of the Lisbon Treaty referendum would appear to offer less tangible, though hotly debated, prizes. No prizes at all, however, offered by NAMA, the new financial wonder, except a handful of inscrutable neologisms: haircut; subordinate bonds; toxic triangle; zombie bank ...

Disappointmint

We have approached all the zoos in the world for a female gorilla for Polo, but none have been forthcoming. Even though this is International Gorilla Year, we have had no luck in finding Polo a mate and it seems highly unlikely that we will. *Vijáyranjan Singh, director of Sri Chamarajendra Zoological Gardens, Mysore, India, on the plight of South Asia's sole surviving male gorilla, born Dublin 1972.*

Rodent inoperative

In all the years that I've done the Liffey Swim I have never seen a rat—or felt one—but there were always stories about them nibbling your toes as you went under O'Connell Bridge. Before they put the green lights in, it was pitch black here. It was low down with a high tide. If you knew at that stage that your chances weren't good, you'd wait around under the bridge and wind up the swimmers by keeping the rat myth alive. *Veteran swimmer Joe Browne.*

Offishial closure

Two cars can't safely pass on the diversion. Our concern is that there will be a fatality. It's so dangerous but now we're told by officials that we'll have to wait as the pinkeens can't be disturbed. It's ridiculous. *Maresa Melvin, spearheading the campaign against the closure of Parkavilla Bridge, Mountrath, Co. Laois.*

YES & NO

The nature of the support for the 'Yes' side is different this time out. Last time, white-collar middle management was into self-expression. This time, they're saying, 'We lose Lisbon, we're fucked.' *PR guru Terry Prone.*

A narrow, bigoted jingoist, peddling an intolerant Little Englander's view of the world. *Minister of State Dick Roche on the intended intervention of Nigel Farage of UKIP (UK Independence Party).*

I presume they'll come over with their imperialist rhetoric. The thought of their smug smiles turns my stomach ... 700 years was enough. *Alan Kelly MEP on UKIP.*

No means Yes
I gave it my best. If there's a 'No' with the cross-party leadership we have in Ireland they'll just make us vote again anyway. No plans to be involved. Waste of time. *Libertas leader Declan Ganley before re-entering the campaign.*

Bed and bored
I stay up nightly, I didn't go to bed at all for the last six months reading the Lisbon Treaty, as I know everybody else in the country is so doing ... Noeleen, my wife, has said to me on repeated occasions, 'Would you ever leave down that Lisbon Treaty and go and make me a cup of tea?' *EU Commissioner Charlie McCreevy.*

Relative values
I'll put it like this. Eighty per cent of what's in the Treaty is good. It's the 20 per cent that gives centralised control to Brussels that I don't like. As a friend of mine put it to me, 'It's like watching an unloved mother-in-law driving over a cliff in your brand-new Mercedes. You like the Mercedes, but you'd bloody love to get rid of the mother-in-law!' *Developer Ulick McEvaddy.*

yes I said yes I will yes

The thing is I think they will keep putting it back at us again if we reject this time and we might as well get it over and done with now. *Co. Cavan farmer Martin Stafford.*

TEANGA BHEO

These proposals are self-destructive both culturally and economically and if implemented could signal the end of 'An Gaeltacht Bheo' as we know it today. The Gaeltacht is not just about our native language; it is about our very culture and heritage. It is our own unique identity and a culture that differentiates us as a nation from the rest of the world. *Broadcaster Mícheál Ó Muircheartaigh on the threat posed by An Bord Snip Nua's recommendation to reduce Gaeltacht funding.*

C no evil

Many people today are shocked at some of the language in Chaucer. *The Canterbury Tales* features the use of the C-word, yet I remember being on the Marian Finucane show a few years back and I tried to talk about its origin and she nearly swooned. *Professor Terry Dolan.*

Signing off

It is such a pity that this was allowed to happen. The signs are very nice but the spelling in Irish is atrocious. There is no way that these signs would be allowed to be put up if the English version was so shoddy. We should have the same standards and respect for our national language. *Translator and Gaeilgeoir Seanán Ó Coistín finds fault with the Historic Town Trail, Naas, Co. Kildare.*

BRICKS & MORTAR

When I came to live in these Ballymun flats 10 years ago, it was more alien than the slums of South America. These were Third World conditions 10 years ago and today they are even worse—especially in the past year or so. The blocks are half-empty, so the gangs have taken over. It's intimidating, it's open to anyone to walk in, there's no security. *Fr Kevin O'Higgins SJ, JUST (Jesuit University Support and Training).*

Vintage port

From here, Parnell made his journeys to Westminster. It was the principal embarkation point for troops departing for the Boer War and the Great War. It was from here that the *Leinster* sailed on its final tragic voyage in October 1918 with over 500 lives lost, and relatives thronging the pier in anxious hope of survivors. Collins, Griffith and their team embarked from the Carlisle Pier to negotiate the Treaty. Old newsreels show Éamon de Valera meeting the Papal Nuncio disembarking for the Eucharistic Congress in 1932. It was also the last Irish building that sheltered many generations of emigrants on their way to an uncertain future. *An Taisce's Ian Lumley protests at the destruction of the Dún Laoghaire pier's former railway station.*

WHERE WE SPORTED & PLAYED

I like watching other sports but when I'm finished, God knows what I'll do then. You can come across footballers who can take it or leave it, it's just a career, but I've never been interested in money. It probably doesn't help to take it so seriously, but what can you do? *Republic of Ireland international Damien Duff.*

Pitch battle

We worked very closely with the Gardaí, who were outstandingly supportive, and our own stewards in trying to create a situation that was going to be to the benefit of all. We thought we were there, after five minutes it looked extremely good, but then we had a break in from Hill 16 and it is impossible to control that. *GAA president Christy Cooney on the Croke Park pitch invasion at the All-Ireland hurling final.*

On Sunday it was exceptionally dangerous at the front of the stage. We had some hairy moments in that crush area as there was no movement there. It became very aggressive, as a lot of boxing and punching went on there. I've a steward with a broken nose and another has an eye injury. *Stadium director Peter McKenny.*

The vast majority of fans only go onto the pitch to see the cup being presented. It's a long-standing tradition. There is absolutely no need to treat them like soccer hooligans. *MEP and former GAA president Seán Kelly.*

Drawing the line

'Peter,' he says, 'there are three things a man should never do: kiss another man's wife, water another man's whiskey—or tie on another man's trout fly.' *Former Ireland soccer manager Jack Charlton quoted by fly-fishing guru Peter O'Reilly.*

Sticky point

It's my view that naming an under-age competition after one of the founders of the Provisional IRA is not appropriate. What I have asked my officials to do is to talk with Sport NI and look at the equality statement all applicants for funding are required to sign and see if we can come to a situation where we can not have commemorations or celebrations of terrorism in sports grounds. *Northern Ireland sports minister Nelson McCausland on the Joe Cahill memorial cup.*

Ireland's call

Even with the prospect of the World Cup it hasn't crossed my mind to come back. I never felt part of the squad and I never will. When I watch Ireland's games it's weird; it's like I was never there. I don't miss it at all, if I'm honest. *Reluctant soccer player Stephen Ireland.*

Plus ça change ...

It feels outstanding! Terrific. Same as it always does. *Kilkenny hurling manager Brian Cody on winning the All-Ireland for the seventh time.*

CÉAD MÍLE FÁILTE

Jack had a real love affair with Ireland. I remember during the planning of his visit to Ireland one of his aides joked with him that the real reason he wanted to go was for a vacation and to have some fun. Jack turned to him and said, 'That's right and I'm going.' He had very warm, close ties with this land, both north and south. *Dan Fenn, founder, JFK Library.*

Clay is the word

It's a rare opportunity we get to come over to Ireland and especially to Ennis. The people of Ennis have been so overwhelming in their outpouring of love for this man and we are sincerely thankful now that we know that Muhammad Ali is an Ennis man; we will be back. *Ali's wife, Lonnie.*

I always heard about this man Cassius Clay, who of course would go on to be Muhammad Ali—my father and brother were mad about him. *Imelda O'Grady, one of Ali's distant Ennis relatives.*

I'm shaking. I never thought for a minute that I would get to meet him. We've had lovely photographs taken with him and I got to kiss him over and over. What can I say, it was unbelievable. *Distant relative Mary O'Donovan.*

This was a pretty difficult visit to organise. We were trying to deal with a number of different aspects. One of them was Mr Ali's personal health, which, from the outset, we said we would do 100 per cent what was required of us in that regard. But with some of the conditions that were being imposed on us, we began to feel that it was making a little bit of a circus of the whole thing. *Ennis Town Manager Ger Dollard.*

NAMARAMA

The Greens have been talking about a social dividend. I believe that NAMA has enough of a job to do to try and resolve the issue that it's been given. *Tom Parlon, Construction Industry Federation.*

I disagree profoundly and fundamentally with him and his members. I have one message for Mr Parlon and his people: 'Please, keep your noses out of NAMA.' *Minister John Gormley.*

Rasher assumption

Do we trust Fianna Fáil and the Minister for Finance to head up the largest property firm on the planet? ... like one of the characters in *Alice in Wonderland,* this legislation requires the public to believe six impossible things before breakfast, all of which come down to a question of trust. *Labour Party finance spokesperson Joan Burton.*

Parish pump

In Donegal, on a small scale, we are living through the consequences of bad decisions. Just look at the situation in relation to water charges, where the council are paying a private company 1 million euro a year to do something that we did for free up to two years ago ... NAMA will have the same effect on us all, except it will be far more expensive and last for generations. *Councillor Thomas Pringle.*

Bail refused

If there is one message I want the House and the citizens of this State to be absolutely clear about, it is that NAMA is not designed to be and will not be permitted to operate as a bail-out mechanism for anybody who has operated irresponsibly. *Taoiseach Brian Cowen.*

SOCIAL & PERSONAL

I can't tell someone if I see something very bad in their future but I would draw attention to the presence of ill-health in the cards. If I see something that is very negative I try to come at it from a philosophical angle and say to the client that life will present challenges and trials and these things will pass. I try to assure them that they won't be in the depths of sorrow or depression for ever. *Tarot consultant Niall O'Connell.*

Shoe-in

When I was young, we used to have stores full of suits, thousands and thousands. They'd all come in on a Monday and take them out of a Friday. When DDT came in they used to spray the suits with it because there'd be fleas on them. In the early '60s the pawn used to be so busy that there was a staff of 13. It was a production line. There'd be one fella for tying up the boxes. Apparently, because a lot of them got on well with the manager, some would put lumps of wood in the boxes but the man presumed there were shoes in them. *Dublin jeweller and pawnbroker Pat Carthy.*

buggermyneighbour

Initially the response was tremendous and we got a lot of feedback and encouragement. However, that petered out and we don't know of anything that's actually ongoing in the public arena as a result of the campaign. I guess people are very busy. *Tom Slattery, Evangelical Alliance of Ireland, on the failure of a campaign launched on loveyourneighbour.ie to persuade people to share acts of kindness.*

Teething troubles

But then again, I also think I'd never have had the capacity to write a book if I hadn't grown up with buck teeth. You weren't picked for the football teams and you didn't kiss girls because no girls wanted to kiss Bugs Bunny, so you read books ... I didn't feel unhappy or distressed. I suppose if I hadn't had that type of lonely childhood, I probably wouldn't have had the capacity to deal with four-and-a-half years staring at a wall the way I did. *Former hostage Brian Keenan.*

Seed and breed

Those men, like my dad, had just come off a farm, and they had grown up milking cattle and growing stuff. But to their children, our generation, it's completely alien. And the next generation down, the grandchildren of the men and women who came from the country in the 1950s and 1960s, are walking around Dundrum with orange faces and UGG boots. To them, farming is a completely foreign world. The memory has gone so quickly. *Journalist Suzanne Campbell.*

Credit rating

I learnt a lot from Simon, about the practicality of help, the solace of company. 'You need food? No problem. You need a hand? It's OK.' I am very grateful. You made my life much more exciting, more focused. I did understand we would still be doing it in 2009 because the reasons for poverty are complex; they are economic and they are political. *Bob Geldof, Simon Community volunteer, 1970.*

PARTY LINES

I was not aware of the cost of these arrangements and when I read the detail in the past weeks I was embarrassed that such costs were associated with some of the arrangements made on my behalf. *Ceann Comhairle John O'Donoghue finally offers a statement on the revelations concerning his expenses while Minister for Arts, Sport and Tourism.*

An honest acknowledgement that some of the expenditure was simply unjustified, an unqualified expression of regret and a forthright apology to the Irish people would have been helpful. *Labour's Róisín Shortall is not impressed.*

There is now a new regime in place in respect of all of that ... What happened in the past was in respect of a regime that was in place at that time. We have to obviously change that regime and that is what we have done. *The Taoiseach clarifies the matter.*

Flagging interest

I received a number of complaints from constituents who attended the Tall Ships event and who told me they were disappointed the Irish navy didn't honour the protocol. One would have hoped that post the Agreement and the new political dispensation, we should have had the maturity to allow that kind of thing to happen without people evading it. *DUP MP Jeffrey Donaldson on the failure of LE* Eithne *to fly the Union Flag at the event.*

Muffled report

There are many recommendations within McCarthy which don't make sense. Many. Many. *Tánaiste Mary Coughlan is less than enthusiastic about some of the prescriptions of An Bord Snip.*

The Opposition would love us to put our two welly boots into it. It's a grand idea to mention welly boots because it's Ploughing Championship week. They're dying for us to do some of the things that McCarthy recommended, because they know they would be totally unacceptable to the people of Ireland. Sorry, Opposition. Not your day. We ain't gonna do them. *Minister Éamon Ó Cuív concurs.*

'ATIN' & DRINKIN'

To think that we can magically inoculate our children against the very toxic drunkenness-tolerant society that we have in Ireland by giving them a glass of wine with Sunday dinner is very naïve, and without any scientific basis. It is children who grew up in families with permissive attitudes and behaviours around alcohol who are much more likely to develop drink and drug problems. *Psychiatrist Bobby Smyth.*

Order in council

There was nothing to put some tea in so I took in a wine glass full of Guinness. It was absolutely a once off—I didn't fancy a glass of water and the next best thing was a glass of Guinness. In hindsight perhaps I shouldn't have done it but it was the most efficient thing to allow the presentation to go ahead. *Banbridge, Co. Down, councillor John Hanna.*

There is a culture where people can go to the fridge and grab a can of beer or a bottle of wine. The practice of drinking before council meetings is totally inappropriate given the fact that we take decisions at these meetings that affect people's lives. *Councillor Dessie Ward.*

Hell's kitchen

If you're at the premier league of your sport and your craft and you have a team of people around you who are all coming to work every day, giving *everything*, the deal is, there is a consequence of bad performance. Call it me giving out, me kicking off, shouting abuse and fuck this and that and the other ... You're talking about bright people here. They're not idiots— you're talking about creative, hard workers at the top of their game. If you're standing in my kitchen with me, if you put up with me for six months, you're fucking good at what you do ... *Dylan McGrath, formerly of Dublin's Mint restaurant.*

LAW & DISORDER

If Sinn Féin is once again sponsoring interface kiddy rioting in order to compete with the dissidents for community control, we are in a very dangerous situation. It would send a strong signal that they have abandoned even the lip service they have paid to the concept of a shared future and settled once more for ghetto politics. *Dr Alasdair McDonnell, SDLP MEP, following sectarian rioting in East Belfast.*

Distant Drumm

I'm telling you now I'm not going to tolerate such nonsense in my courtroom. If I want Professor Brendan Drumm himself in my courtroom, I will issue a warrant to bring him here if I have to. Let it be very clear that I will not tolerate this type of bureaucratic behaviour. When it comes to the welfare of children this court will not stop until all matters are investigated thoroughly. *Judge John Neilan takes a strong line.*

Cut above

The Romanians—they'll stick a knife in you as soon as look at you. There might be some good ones. By gosh, some of those European ones, they make the Irish look like complete amateurs. *Leicester councillor Robert Fraser.*

ARTS & PARTS

The biggest loss to me personally is my increasing inability to draw because it is my drawing and writing hand that is affected most by the disorder. Not being able to draw a straight line is not funny when you are an artist. I had to let go of my calligraphy and illustration. Working on copperplate also became impossible. I also had to let go of the precise movements that were required to design book covers. And although I had retired, I was still called on to do such work. Slowly I had to change. I had to find new ways of expressing my creativity. *Jan de Fouw, afflicted with Parkinson's disease.*

Juden raus

But these Jews, these fucking Jews come up to me. Fucking Christ-killing bastards. Fucking six million? I would have got 10 or 12 million out of that, no fucking problem. Two at a time, they would have gone. Held hands, get in there. Leave us your teeth and your glasses. *Comedian Tommy Tiernan.*

He quite clearly brought to the surface his own prejudices and what he said is more a commentary on his own personal prejudices and perspectives. Rather than this being a comic presentation, it sounds more like the deranged, demented ramblings of a complete fool, which I don't think reasonable people would remotely take seriously. *Alan Shatter TD.*

I can only decry the comments as insensitive and hurtful to the suffering of victims and to a memory which is sacred. Comedy does not bring with it unlimited licence. Comedy can easily become the forerunner of intolerance. Indeed, comedy can be subtly dressed up to be cruel and to show disregard. Trivialisation of the Holocaust can be as hurtful as denial. *Archbishop Diarmuid Martin.*

Old flames

I think people are sick of hearing the Daniel O'Donnell-type songs about mothers' hearts falling into the fire and four country roads. *Singer and accordionist Séamus Begley.*

Art of what we are

Of all the things that have helped to brand Ireland over the years, many of them have taken a hammering, but culture and the imagination haven't.

We've a great opportunity to show what we can do: it's not about throwing more money at it, it's about showing off what we have already. *Dermot McLaughlin, Temple Bar Culture Trust, Dublin.*

I taught for 20 years and in every class of 20 or 30 children you always get three or four of a sensitive artistic bent. So what are they to do? Stand in the corner and feel shamed again? The point is that if Ireland is proud of its heritage, it will have to accept that artists are role models every bit as much as sportspeople. *Author Patrick McCabe on the Bord Snip threat to the funding of arts and artists.*

One of the things I found most peculiar in their argument about the abolition of this tax concession was if it was removed, artists would continue anyway. I found that an extraordinary argument. It's a bit like saying if we halve the wages of nurses or teachers, sure, they will keep on working anyway ... *Artist and designer Robert Ballagh.*

It enables artists to survive on or above the breadline for long enough to establish themselves in the marketplace of creativity. Still, I get a pain in my arse listening to some of their spokespeople going on about the indispensability of the artistic community, as though its worth was self-evident and implying that it is obvious that the country owes them something. *Journalist and writer John Waters.*

The fact that we have such a strong culture as a country really gives us one of the big advantages of any nation in the world. We are famous for our writers, our artists, our poets, and we are not famous for much else. *Businessman Denis O'Brien.*

Fond farewell
I wanted to be the first to tell you. It's the least I owe you, for endless years, countless hours of morning companionship, friendship, good humour and laughter. Your loyalty and support has been a beacon of love in my life. *Terry Wogan takes leave of his loyal BBC radio audience.*

WAR & PEACE

I want to know—and the victims are entitled to know—why Gordon Brown does not have the same desire to stand up for the victims of IRA terrorism as George Bush shows standing up for American victims. *Jeffrey Donaldson MP.*

We see Libya rejoicing over the return of al-Megrahi and the Scottish government was, in my opinion, right to show compassion to a dying man. But I think it's now time for Libya to acknowledge the pain and suffering they inflicted by supporting the IRA and show the same compassion to its victims. *Colin Parry, whose son was killed in the IRA bombing of Warrington, Cheshire.*

Gaddafi provided the weapons but the triggers were pulled, the bombs planted and the murder undertaken by people much closer to home. *Ulster Unionist leader Sir Reg Empey.*

Go to the Irish-Americans who were giving them money to buy arms. *Libyan Minister for European Affairs Abdulati Alobidi on the suggestion that Libya should pay restitution to IRA victims killed with weapons supplied by that country.*

You couldn't write the script for this; if you did it would be *Monty Python*. Here we have the police helping out the people who trained the IRA and supplied the weapons to murder their colleagues. It's just unbelievable. *William Frazer, IRA victims' organisation FAIR, on the PSNI officers' Libyan training assignment.*

It is clear from the reception for the Lockerbie bomber that Libya still has a long way to go. Consequently none of our elected representatives will be supporting any future deployment of police personnel to Libya until they have reached a settlement on the payment of compensation to PIRA victims and relations have been normalised. *First Minister Peter Robinson.*

HERE & THERE

The farmers are back in vogue this year. The women place great value on the farming community and the likes of the building contractors would not be as popular as other years. A builder could build you 100 houses, but at the moment, who would want them? But you can't make an acre; there is great security in the land. At times like this, it stands out. *Matchmaker Willie Daly at the Lisdoonvarna Matchmaking Festival, Co. Clare.*

There & here

I used to work with this old Israeli guy. He did business all over the world and he used to say that no matter where he went in the world to do business there were always Irish and Jews sitting at the end of the table. He asked me, 'What do you do with your Irish abroad? Our best resource is the fact that we have Jews all over the world.' *Economist David McWilliams explains how he conceived the idea of the Global Economic Forum.*

Ireland has to look farther east. It needs to look at China, at the Middle East, at south-east Asia. *James Hogan, chief executive, Etihad airline, at the Forum.*

We know you are busy people. And yet, when asked, you put your own preoccupations aside and came to Dublin to share your wisdom and experience with us as we try to construct a pathway through today's economic difficulties to a sustainably prosperous future for our people. *President Mary McAleese thanks participating members of the Forum held at Farmleigh, Dublin.*

Up in arms

The people of this town are proud of their heritage; they are proud of their history; they are proud that they have a municipal Council that dates back almost four centuries and they are proud of the coat of arms of this Borough. I think it is time that we told the County Manager that he will have to respect this Council, that he will have to respect the democratic decisions of this Council and that he will have to respect the history and heritage of this town. *Sligo Borough councillor Declan Bree on the proposal to replace the town arms.*

Snoblesse oblige

There was absolute uproar over it. Templeogue and Terenure were going to leave Ranelagh and have their post delivered out of Kimmage instead of Rathmines. At first, they were going to be designated Dublin 26 but there was a huge fuss over that because it was too close to the postal code for Tallaght and Jobstown, which was 24. Then, a compromise was reached and we came up with Dublin 6W (West) in 1985. Even now, there are still about 200 people who cannot accept they are part of Dublin 6W and refuse to use it. It's a fantastic example of snobbery. *Dublin postman Cormac Ó Dálaigh.*

Current affair

I'm a very strong swimmer. I swim in the Barrow all the time. It wasn't dangerous, but we knew what we were at. We meant to go from A to B, but with the current, we ended up at Z. The water was freezing—it took us about 15 minutes to get to the other side. Afterwards, we had a magnificent picnic in Scotland. I've always wanted to swim from one country to another. *Green Party TD Mary White conquers the Tweed.*

Trackless waste

I always compare Donegal's position in Ireland to Siberia's in Russia with one difference. Siberia has a train servicing it. *Playwright Frank McGuinness.*

CHURCH & STATE

He came to halt the slide to materialism and secularism and apparently he gave the bishops a right bollocking behind the scenes. There was a lot of talk about Ireland as the jewel in the Catholic crown, but it was the same year we'd prepared our first legislation regarding contraception, which went totally against the Vatican encyclical of the late '60s. *Historian Diarmaid Ferriter recalling the visit of Pope John Paul II in 1979.*

I was part of a group called Irish Women United. They opposed the visit. I did not. They opposed it because of the Pope's stand on women's issues and contraception. Their protests mainly took the form of abstentionism. Given Irish history back to the penal laws and back to Cromwell, I was quite determined to see him. For those historical reasons, but also because I'd never seen a pope before. And it was one of the great highlights of my life. *Writer Nell McCafferty.*

With great relief, I burst into the toilet, only to discover it was the dining room where the Pope was taking his lunch. Luckily I had not proceeded to divest myself in any fashion. The shock put any need to go to the toilet out of my head ... Cardinal Ó Fiaich said to me, 'Brian, come in. Eat the Pope's dinner, sit on the Pope's chair, because it's the only time you'll ever get near it.' *Fr Brian Darcy.*

Clerical erer

I don't leave with any sense of grievance whatsoever. I'm leaving because I feel there's so much more to be done. Put it like this, there are plenty of Presbyterian ministers, Methodists and Roman Catholic priests. We have a fair abundance of clerics. But I don't think we have enough artists who are coming from a sense of wanting to celebrate people's lives. *Belfast Presbyterian minister Keith Drury embraces a new career.*

$E = M[ARY] \, C[OUGHLAN]^2$

... like Einstein explaining his theory of evolution. *An Tánaiste gets her theories crossed.*

Thank you, Ireland

—says José Manuel Barroso, President of the European Commission, on learning of the outcome of the re-run referendum: 'It's a great day for Ireland and a great day for Europe. I want to congratulate the Irish people on reaching their overwhelming decision after such long and careful deliberation.' John O'Donoghue is made to carry the can for all those involved in the political expenses scandal, and the month ends, predictably, with Halloween, which, according to Justin Parr of Miss Fantasia, 'is not just a children's event any more. For adults, this time of year is about indulging in fantasies and when better to explore your sexuality than when you're dressed up or masked …'

Tá

What happened in Ireland was that they got the littlest boy in the playground and put him in the corner and have given him a good kicking. *Nigel Farage, UKIP (UK Independence Party).*

This was a mature vote in which the Irish people rejected those voices telling them to make the referendum a verdict on the government and on national policies. The voters also resisted the Trojan horses which were wheeled into this country bearing British Eurosceptics, like the United Kingdom Independence Party, the Open Europe think-tank and the British-owned anti-European media. *Pat Cox, Yes group Ireland for Europe.*

For a small country, we have left our mark on the Lisbon Treaty, as we did on the Nice Treaty. We have got our Irish solution to our Irish problem. This is not something to boast about, as it reflects an attitude that is ambiguous, inward-looking and instinctively questions the motives of others. *Labour Party TD Joe Costello.*

Catch 33

It's actually a story of a peninsula beside a border. The people of Inishowen feel they are the 33rd county of Ireland and this is a statement that they are not happy with the government ... The sound of Donegal's No vote must ring around the negotiating room in Brussels when stakeholders sit down to thrash out a new fisheries deal. *Fine Gael TD Joe McHugh on Donegal's unique No vote.*

It's a grubby victory for the elite who spent enormous sums frightening and manipulating people. *Cóir's Richard Greene.*

Well, there won't be a Lisbon Three, that's for sure. *Taoiseach Brian Cowen.*

LESSER BREEDS

The rams race 100 metres and I like to include some hurdles as they are great jumpers ... Flat racing can be a little boring! We've had great interest in them; there is usually a clear winner, although we've had a few photo finishes. *Co. Roscommon farmer Matt O'Dowd on one of the attractions of Pet Expo, part of World Animal Week.*

Cause for llamantation

I was very surprised to see them gone. Whoever took them walked them a considerable distance until they got them to the roadway ... I can't understand why anyone would want to steal them. *Joe Moran, pound owner, Summerhill, Co. Meath, laments the disappearance of circus llamas found wandering on the Red Cow Roundabout and impounded by South Dublin County Council.*

It began with kangaroos; then it was camels. At some stage there was an elephant; now apparently it's llamas. It's cheap. It's inhumane. It's unnecessary. *Charles O'Brien, Fossett's Circus, on the alleged practice of allowing circus animals to escape for publicity purposes.*

Full Monty

We already have a guy who has a 3.6 metre python in a box bedroom and the only way he can feed it is to throw food through the window because he's afraid of it as it's got so big. This year alone the DSPCA has taken in five bearded dragons, a blue tree frog, one iguana, monitor lizards, brown American squirrels, numerous terrapins and 15 snakes. *Jimmy Cahill, Dublin Society for the Prevention of Cruelty to Animals, laments the lack of legislation governing exotic animals.*

Frise frame

People look in the local paper, they see an ad for a bichon frise puppy, so they ring up and a friendly woman says that she'll bring the pup and meet them at the roundabout at the end of the motorway, so they don't have to travel so far. Then, if they like the puppy, they can take him there and then. The people standing holding their new puppy at the roundabout see only the cute, fluffy tip of the iceberg. *David Wilson, USPCA (Ulster Society for the Prevention of Cruelty to Animals), on the trade in farmed puppies.*

A LITTLE LEARNING

We are a society of amateurs. There are some professional historians among us but not that many and the amateurs provide a slant on the ordinary life of Dublin, the life of John Citizen if you like, that the professional doesn't always have time to do. *Rev. Dudley Levistone Cooney, president, Old Dublin Society.*

Chain reaction

We didn't agree with the introduction of fees but we suggested a student contribution. However, this document will send Irish education down the toilet, and it is clear now that, given he put all his eggs in one basket, this is a resigning issue for Batt O'Keeffe. *Fine Gael TD Brian Hayes upbraids the Minister for Education.*

Schools out

What is at stake are 21 schools serving the Protestant community, some hundreds of years old, which are supported by a large number of people who wish to exercise their right to be educated within their own ethos. *Archbishop of Dublin John Neill objects to the proposed reclassification of Protestant schools.*

It would be a shame in the days, post Good Friday agreement and St Andrews when we're working hard throughout Ireland to recognise minority rights and encourage everyone to play their part in the State, that a minority down here are discriminated against and are not able at school to reflect the Christian ethos that their parents wish. *Presbyterian Minister Trevor D. Gribben.*

Are we seriously to believe that the founding fathers and framers of our Constitution envisaged a situation where this republic would become a hostile place for the children of the Protestant minority? *Bishop of Cork Paul Colton.*

I believe there is a public interest in guaranteeing the right of the Protestant community to education ... Without the Protestant communities and without their schools I believe Ireland today, or pluralism in Ireland, would be poorer. *Archbishop of Dublin Diarmuid Martin.*

Re Kindling

There is some international evidence of falling patterns of reading generally. In a sense, that's a separate problem, but it's a problem that is potentially compounded by things like the Kindle. But it is also a problem that is possibly ameliorated by the Kindle, if you can deliver reading to a generation that takes the screen as a default. *Publisher Fergal Tobin.*

Road to Rome

We may well ask, where does the Catholic education highway lead? Are we satisfied that it has become almost inevitable that the individual's education is to be completed at a state college or university? If we believe that Catholic education is a lifelong process of human growth and development, including spiritual growth, is it not important that we have a Catholic presence as part of the diversity of the third-level sector? *Dr Peadar Cremin, Mary Immaculate College of Education, Limerick.*

PARTY LINES

A Cheann Comhairle, I regret to say this but I consider that your position is no longer tenable. I think you will either have to resign or I think you will have to be removed from office and, following the order of business today, it is my intention to meet my colleagues in the Labour parliamentary party and to recommend to them the tabling of a motion of no confidence in you. *Labour Party leader Eamon Gilmore.*

Thank you, Deputy Gilmore. *Ceann Comhairle John O'Donoghue.*

What's another ear?

Eamon Gilmore got the head of John O'Donoghue, and what Fine Gael is trying to do now is to get the left ear of his decapitated head. Will you for heaven's sake stop flogging the head of a dead horse? *Jim McDaid TD.*

As I say, there are some who can't step back from dancing on a grave, and I'm not one of them. *Taoiseach Brian Cowen.*

We are all devastated by it. We don't think it is a fair reflection of him. We feel he has been scapegoated. We think it is a bit unfair that he had been singled out on his own. He is devastated and terribly hurt, as we all are. *John O'Donoghue's brother Paul.*

Even in darkest Africa they'd give some fella some sort of a trial before they'd execute him. Jesus, even back in the time of the Black and Tans they'd nearly give a fella some bit of a trial before they'd hang him. *Former South Kerry TD and Minister of State John O'Leary.*

I came into this House an honest man. I never asked anything of any man. I never took anything from any man. I never could. I never would. To do otherwise would be to deny who I am and who I came from. I will walk proudly out of this chair, as proud as the day I walked into it. *John O'Donoghue.*

No show

I have to record my annoyance at the fact I have not been able to develop a close working relationship with Peter Robinson. That is through no deficiency or lack of effort on my part. *Deputy First Minister Martin McGuinness.*

The deputy should try and control himself, especially when in public. *First Minister Peter Robinson.*

Upper cut

I believe the Seanad should be abolished and the next Fine Gael government will put this to the people. I have come to the conclusion that a second house of the Oireachtas can no longer be justified. *Fine Gael leader Enda Kenny.*

Not to put a tooth in it

The Seanad is of systematic importance to the Constitution as there are several references to the Seanad. There are a number of references that are all interlocked. So, to use a dental analogy, to abolish the Seanad would not be a constitutional filling and more full root canal treatment with a few extractions. *Dr Gerard Hogan, Trinity College Dublin.*

If he asked my advice, which he didn't, I would have said, 'Look, find something where people are really concerned, like perhaps house repossession, or something that would have got to people to say, "This is what Fine Gael thinks and can do for you."' *Former Fine Gael minister Nora Owen.*

If the Seanad was abolished in the morning that would be one less voice for Waterford. I have mixed feelings, to be quite honest. *Fine Gael Senator Paudie Coffey (Waterford).*

No swine flew

I'm 65 years old. I do not anticipate seeing pigs in flight but I'm very grateful that I've lasted long enough to see turkeys voting for Christmas. *Independent Senator David Norris.*

LAW & DISORDER

He was walking in a very peculiar manner and appeared that he had a hockey stick concealed down the leg of his tracksuit pants. He was intoxicated and very agitated. I managed to get the hockey stick and I placed it in the patrol car. When I began to get details from him, he became extremely aggressive and agitated and he told me it would be best if I fucked off. *Cork garda Timothy Walsh.*

Matter of forms

I think bureaucracy can be a very helpful comfort blanket. You can show success by filling in a form well—that doesn't necessarily mean you are doing the things that matter. When the bureaucracy takes you away from having the space and time to deal with victims appropriately, then the bureaucracy must be wrong. *Chief Constable Matt Baggott, PSNI.*

Police statement

Now, we know what it means to be supportive and we also know what it means to meddle. And I want to be clear that when it comes to the important issue of devolution, of policing and justice, that is a decision for this Assembly to make. *US Secretary of State Hillary Clinton in Belfast.*

Not one single business figure has ever said to me, 'I am holding off investing in Northern Ireland because the devolution of policing powers to the Assembly has not happened yet.' *Industry minister Arlene Foster.*

I have never met any inward investor who has come either from New York or Johannesburg or anywhere else who gets off the plane in Belfast, goes to Invest NI and says, 'Well, what's the policing and justice situation like here?' It just does not happen. *DUP MP Gregory Campbell.*

MAMMON

I knew that public sector wages were high in Ireland but I never dreamt they were this high. I was offered 50 per cent more than I was earning at Hamburg University. At this stage, the truth is I don't know how much I earn. I get paid too much; it's ridiculous. *Dutch professor Richard Tol, ESRI (Economic and Social Research Institute).*

Auto suggestions

If you think about it, the last thing you're going to do in a recession, if your car is still getting you from A to B, is buy a car. Back in the good old Celtic Tiger days, you had to be seen with your '07 or your '08 car. Was that logical? If you go to Germany or France they didn't have that obsession with having to change your car. Maybe we do have to question that. Why are we so status conscious? *Minister John Gormley.*

There was no limo in Wales. A limo conjures up an image of a long, sleek vehicle, you know, and people drinking cocktails in the back of it. This was a people carrier. The only way we could get to the venue was by car. *John Gormley, arís, on not taking the train from Holyhead to Hay-on-Wye.*

Gone the time

About an hour and a half—they're all broke. *Economist Colm McCarthy, asked how long a tax on developers would keep the country going.*

PLAYING THE GAME

I described it to someone as me managing Leitrim against France—not just that, but if Leitrim was scattered around 18 islands out in the middle of the sea, where they had no near neighbours who could play them in games. *Faroe Islands soccer coach Brian Kerr.*

Horse & jockey

He is probably, after 300 years of bloodstock breeding, the ultimate development of the thoroughbred horse. He has got great pedigree and great looks and great athleticism and size and a great ability over a variety of distances. You could not hope to breed a better horse and he represents the ultimate development of the bloodstock industry here. *Trainer John Oxx on flat-race champion Sea the Stars.*

Racing in Ireland isn't an everyday grind, and it would have been impossible to have a proper family life in England. Here, I have the perfect balance. And I'm happy. If I don't leave the place here for five or six days, I'm happy just labouring away. England is different. Yes, the people that offered me the jobs appealed, but not the life. *Sea the Stars' jockey Mick Kinane.*

It was a great privilege to have been there. I felt it was an utterly exceptional performance as for the first time in his career, the atmosphere really got to him. *Racing commentator Peter O'Sullevan on watching Sea the Stars win the Prix de l'Arc de Triomphe.*

Home turf

I was looking out at the rain one day while on the phone to a friend, and told him that even the bog was flooded. He said I should look up 'bog snorkelling', so I did. I found that there were championships in Northern Ireland and in Wales, but none here. In January I got into the bog in my tracksuit—I didn't even have a wetsuit at the time—with flippers and snorkel. My son posted it on YouTube and the response was amazing. Before we knew it we had 48 competitors, including a hen party from the UK. *Declan Connolly, Alice's Loft and Cottages, Castleblayney, Co. Monaghan.*

Cutting his cloth

We must remember that we have different material to work with—Italy have silk, whereas I only have cotton. *Republic of Ireland coach Giovanni Trapattoni after the draw with Italy.*

A travesty, a terrible performance, shameful. *Commentator Eamon Dunphy after the same match.*

Dunphy, he should know better by now. He's a skinny rat, a skinny little rat. *International Stephen Hunt.*

Conkering hero

I'll just have to try and keep my feet on the ground and not let this incredible achievement go to my head. *Alison Dooley, Freshford, Co. Kilkenny, winner of the Conker Championship Cup.*

AG OBAIR

My first night on the job I was on the rescue unit, and they sent me to help get a body out of the Liffey. The man had been missing for months. He'd fallen off a ship and the sea had given up its dead. When the lads dragged his body in, I nearly threw up. It was 10 times its normal size because it was so bloated and all the skin comes off when you take it out of the water. I watched the skin just float away like a glove. I'll never forget that night, but you do learn to deal with it. You have to. *Paddy Hughes, Dublin Fire Brigade.*

Bloody but uncowed

In our business, every year there's something. This year it's a global credit crunch; before, it was mad cow or 9/11 or some guy decided to shoot somebody or war breaks out. There's always some challenge. *Darryl Ismail, Chase Travel International, Malahide, Co. Dublin.*

Rocha and a hard place

It's hard to have a fashion business in any country, but even more difficult in Ireland. It has been a lot of ups and downs, as we all know, but I had a vision when I first came here, to base myself here and to create what I create from this country. And sell it to the rest of the world. I didn't realise it would take me 30 years! *Fashion designer John Rocha.*

Table for two

RTÉ didn't fire. You would have had to have done something terrible to the director-general's wife on the canteen table in the nude to get fired. *Former RTÉ producer and controller of programmes John Kelleher.*

TEANGA BHEO

When I moved back to Cork, I became interested in place-names, particularly around my father and mother's countryside, beautiful names like Tír na Spideoige, or land of the robin. This interest drew me back into the language. *Radio presenter John Creedon.*

Royal charter

Promoting the language is very important. We do not want our children to grow up and have a crisis of identity. In five to ten years there will be 40,000 Igbo people in Ireland. We are teaching our children that they are Irish and Nigerian. Integration is very important and we also want to live by our own culture here. *His Royal Highness eze Matthew Emeka Ezeani, eze Igbo of Ireland.*

Grandmother tongue

My grandmother had a great love of Irish, but she would switch to English just to communicate. I suppose one has to draw inspiration from the men and women involved in the political and cultural renaissance which helped form the State. The idealism and their view of the language as part of our landscape and heritage is as valid now as it was back them. *Nuacht anchorwoman Siún Nic Gearailt.*

Beidh law eile

It appears that many Irish speakers, even in the strongest Gaeltacht areas, are either unaware of their right to use Irish in court business or remain convinced that it is in their best interests to leave their language rights and preferences aside and opt for English as the default language of the law. *Seán Ó Cuirreáin, An Coimisinéir Teanga.*

BRICKS & MORTAR

Like all small boys I didn't look at buildings. I was in Dublin between the ages of eight and 13 and I can give you first-hand testimony that kids do not give a great deal of attention to architecture. I became more interested bit by bit. *Architectural historian Maurice Craig.*

Back to his route

I want to thank everyone from the design team who put it right behind my back door. I'm probably the only person who they could see wouldn't be objecting to it. *Taoiseach Brian Cowen opens the adjacent Tullamore bypass.*

Stone fad

Unique and vulnerable habitats are being destroyed by visitors when they illegally remove protected limestone pavement to build the dolmens ... It is only recently that the erection of these dolmens has become a fad. *Carol Gleeson, Burren Connect project.*

Relics and aul' decency

In those days if you said your dad was an architect it would be like saying now that he was an archaeologist. It was a gentleman's profession, it wasn't about money. Money was considered to be a vulgar 'add-on' to the architecture. My father didn't see it as a business, and he never cultivated the politicians and developers. *Architect David Collins.*

Extra ordinary

I was never able to do what a lot of ordinary people were able to do, buy houses in France, Spain and Italy and buy houses down the country. I find it hard enough to have one house and very ordinary people in this country can afford to do a lot better than that. *Former Taoiseach Bertie Ahern.*

SOCIAL & PERSONAL

Domestic violence is calculated to control and destroy the human spirit. I would like to be able to tell you we are making significant progress to eradicate this violence, but I cannot. What I will tell you is that services are being cut back all the time by this government, that services are stretched and cannot stretch any more. *Sharon O'Halloran, Safe Ireland.*

Mé féin

I don't like being alone. I'm a people person. I live by myself so it doesn't get more bachelor than that. It's not a novelty any more. *RTÉ presenter Gerry Ryan.*

The older you get, the worse it gets, no doubt about it—unless you choose to be alone, like monks or other non-religious people. But if you haven't chosen to be alone, it gets worse and I think Irish society is very insensitive towards things like loneliness, depression and suicide. *Poet Paul Durcan.*

ARTS & PARTS

There is a suggestion that to be an Irish writer is to be engaged with nature and Irishness, and that's what defines an Irish writer. I suppose the question that one then asks is, well, what if you *don't* want to engage with Irishness? What do you then become? *Novelist John Connolly.*

Getting there by degrees

The Chieftains were part-time back then so we were still trying to make it as musicians. There wouldn't have been a lot of money and it was only when Gay Byrne attended the honorary ceremony for the honorary doctorate that Trinity gave me that my mother realised I had a real career. *Paddy Moloney remembers the early days.*

Shooting gallery

The new Troubles gallery is tentative. We are trying to give a headline sense of the key issues here. But you can't resolve this stuff. People might expect a definitive exhibition. The impact of the Troubles is unresolved—so the gallery is unresolved. *Tim Cooke, National Museums Northern Ireland, on the new Ulster Museum initiative.*

Different drum

Symphony orchestra players do everything. Sometimes you're asked to play coconut shells, or break glasses. As a professional in the business, it has become harder for us, in that you're expected to know about everything. You might arrive in to do a soundtrack recording and someone says, 'Oh, we want you to play a doumbeck.' *Percussionist Noel Eccles.*

FAITH & MORALS

From beginning to end Ian Paisley never shook my hand. His wife would but Ian Paisley wouldn't because I was a Catholic. Of course, Tony wasn't Catholic at the time. *Cherie Blair, wife of the former British Prime Minister.*

Orange aura

I saw in the deeds that Richard Dawson Bates had lived in this house for around 30 or 40 years. He was an absolute bigot and he hated Catholics with a passion. He was a chain smoker and we've all smelt smoke in this house even though none of us smoke. I was wondering is it him, because we're the first Catholic family ever to have lived in this house. *Nathan Fitzpatrick on the apparent haunting of his Belfast house by a former Unionist politician and Minister for Home Affairs.*

When they said about smoke—that is one type of infestation that is quite common—smells of perfume or tobacco. I first worked with this family five years ago and after some advice I gave them, it all stopped. But it has started again, so I'm going to see what is needed. I hope this man is not going to hold it against me for coming over because I'm a Roman Catholic too. *American demonologist Lorraine Warren.*

Belittled People

We have changed over time. There was a time when nine out of 10 Irish people would believe in fairies; nowadays you'd be lucky to get one out of 10. Those that do believe in fairies and the like are afraid to admit it in case people laugh at them. *Folklorist Margaret Humphries, University College, Cork.*

Knock and they shall be opened ...

She will rock the foundations of the Church if the people do not listen, from Rome back to down where we are, down to Knock. And the gates of heaven will be closed. She says she'll do it. *The Blessed Virgin Mary, as reported by clairvoyant Joe Coleman, predicting a visitation at the Mayo shrine.*

It is not healthy, does not give glory to God and certainly is not good witness to the faith, to be looking for extraordinary phenomena ... The shrine of Knock will be best served by retaining its authentic identity. *Archbishop Michael Neary.*

Honest broker

The economy may screw you, but God won't. He is always there. *Fr Michael Cusack, Dundalk.*

HIS & HERS

Senator David Norris could very well be our first openly gay presidential candidate. That would be a test issue. It would be similar to the candidacy of Mary Robinson in 1990. Her gender was second to her manifest other abilities, but, for some, it was still a factor. *Ruairí Quinn TD.*

Not in your wellies

Women have been invisible for far too long in agriculture and we want to see an end to that day and for the place of women in agriculture, agribusiness and across the sector generally to be acknowledged. *Mairéad Lavery, Agri Aware.*

We have decided to let a Dubliner in but the female thing is still a definite no. We based that on the fact that the ICA [Irish Countrywomen's Association] refuses male members and until they drop that, neither will we. *Paddy Rock, organiser of the Original Irish Culchie Festival.*

'ATIN' & DRINKIN'

People say after one drink it lessens your concentration or whatever or you're not as good a driver or you're not able to drive. I don't really accept that. I mean, that can be argued the other way as well. Some people, a drink, if it's such a sedative, it can make people who're, you know, jumpy on the road or nervous, can be more relaxed. All these arguments can be argued both ways. *Mattie McGrath TD on the proposal to reduce the permitted blood alcohol level for drivers from 80 mg to 50 mg per 100 ml.*

For and a Guinness

You'll always have at least two sides at meetings. The same ones who want to allow a drink to the poor aul' fellas who want to drive home will also be on about one-off housing and farm benefits. They see themselves as the oppressed, the victims of an attack on rural culture by the D4s—'You're all agin us'. *Séamus Boland, Irish Rural Link.*

It's the poor fella that calls in for a pint and a half on the way home from the likes of Castleisland or Kenmare Mart: that's who I'm looking out for. If he's stopped then he'd be totally isolated and he's not one to buy beer or whiskey for the home. That's not what he's about. *Jackie Healy-Rae TD.*

If rural Ireland is dependent on us allowing people to get into a car with an excess of alcohol in their blood, put themselves or other road-users in danger, then rural Ireland has come to a sorry state. *Minister Noel Dempsey.*

Even five years ago, you'd hear of people who would boast about how much they had to drink the night before and yet drove into work that morning. That sort of talk just wouldn't be seen as acceptable in many workplaces today. *Noel Brett, Road Safety Authority.*

From Clare to here
The weirdest place I've ever seen a McPub is in Dubai. It was so hot they had air conditioning units the size of jet turbines ... This enormous expense to create the homely sense of a small Burren bar. It was just like Ennistymon, but 40 degrees hotter. '*Lonely Planet' writer Fionn Davenport.*

Not on the manu
One of the older chefs told me that when he went to a dance he couldn't tell a girl that he cooked for a living because it wasn't manly. *Chef Máirtín Mac Con Iomaire.*

Allah carte
You read a lot about the Michelin Guide and when you meet one of the inspectors it's like meeting God. *Georgina O'Sullivan, Ballymore Inn, Ballymore Eustace, Co. Wicklow.*

HERE & THERE

It was extremely difficult for both of us. We were constantly fearing for our lives, especially in the initial stages when there were constant threats and intimidation. We weren't sure at all if we were going to get out alive in those first months. After a while we became more hopeful, but there were mood swings because you would be paralysed with fear over what was going to happen next. *Sharon Commins, Goal worker held hostage in Darfur.*

You're made of tough stuff. *President Mary McAleese.*

This is the truth. Had I not intervened though these mediations, this situation couldn't have been sorted out like this. These guys would not have killed the girls but they would have taken them to Chad or any other place. *Musa Hilal, special adviser to the Sudanese president, claims a ransom was paid.*

When the former president Mary Robinson came back from a visit to Darfur-Chad her description of what she saw and heard made her quite emotional. I should say if you ask Irish people, then and now, where should the Defence Forces go it would be Chad-Darfur. *Defence Forces Chief of Staff Lieutenant-General Dermot Earley.*

Unkindest cut

I ended up dangling upside down from a rope attached to a guy called Paul Clerkin. And yes, he considered cutting it. With the fall I'd taken, he assumed I was dead. He had the weight of me and all my equipment slowly suffocating him. He was rummaging for his penknife. Luckily, I managed to get upright and get a foothold in the rock. *Climber Terence 'Banjo' Bannon remembers a bad day on Ben Nevis.*

OH YEH?

The best line I ever wrote was a 'Yeh'. *Playwright Billy Roche.*

After the referee decides, the game is feenish for me

—*says manager Giovanni Trapattoni (as transliterated by Irish Times journalist Kathy Sheridan), in the wake of that infamous 'Main de Dieu' World Cup incident in Paris: 'I know it is imposseebil to replay the game.' Others are not so philosophically detached. 'It's up to the French,' says the FAI's John Delaney: 'Their president actually said to me afterwards that it was a handball and if I was Thierry Henry, I wouldn't like to be remembered like Maradona. If they came out and said that they would accede to a replay then I think that FIFA would go with that.' They didn't.*

He said he hadn't intended to, it had just happened. He's admitted that he cheated and that we should have gone through. He didn't apologise but he admitted it. What can you do, though? That's the result now and they've gone through. *Defender Richard Dunne.*

If it was at the other end and an Irishman did it, we'd acknowledge it, and take it. I'm not justifying it. It was a foul and it's gone against Ireland, but anyone would have done it. *Commentator Jim Beglin.*

I'd be more annoyed with my defenders and my goalkeeper than Thierry Henry. How can you leave a ball bounce in the six-yard box? How can you let Thierry Henry get goalside of you? If the ball bounces in the six-yard box, I'd be saying, 'Where the hell is my goalkeeper?' *Former Ireland captain Roy Keane.*

Transformation seen
This has never been done before in the history of stadiums. Really it is a 14-hour timeline from the end of the match until the corporate turnstiles

open at 12.30 the next day. The intention is for the public arriving for the rugby match to feel like the previous day never happened. *Croke Park operations manager Alan Gallagher on a tight transition.*

But we won't have a spare second. We've never contemplated doing something so ambitious before—to convert an international soccer pitch into an international rugby pitch overnight. *Stadium director Peter McKenna. (France beat Ireland in the soccer; Ireland drew with Australia in the rugby.)*

Opening up Croke Park has been shown to be the right decision. We have seen the benefit in the GAA and in my opinion Central Council should now be given the right to decide on the future of the stadium. *GAA Director-General Paraic Duffy.*

Distant Drums

I had been in the dressing rooms before with my father when he was manager of Drumcondra. That was as close as I had ever got. That day of my debut was like living in a dream. I left home as a boy in 1956 to go to Manchester United as a 15-year-old. Now here I was, home, three years later and ready to play for Ireland. *John Giles remembers.*

Poc fada

He is the first openly gay Irish hurler since Cú Chulainn. *Author Colm Tóibín on Dónal Óg Cusack.*

End game

The one thing about bridge is that you can be sure of a good funeral. *Rita Cassidy, North Munster bridge secretary, on the camaraderie of the cards.*

CALLS OF NATURE

We wondered, what if you crossed a cow and a pig? Would it be stable? So, we designed a pig-cow hybrid on the computer and called it a pow. It says 'moink'. *Young Scientist Derek Rice, Ardscoil Éanna, Dublin.*

The waters and the wild

Lough Derg is filling faster than we can empty it and the nature of the Shannon is such that it is a long, meandering, flat water body which takes weeks to discharge itself. The combination of such heavy rain, together with the fact that extensive development has taken place, much of it on flood plains, means that we are in a situation that we have not had since records began. *ESB's Michael McNicholas.*

There was a flood in the month of May which washed away birds' nests and straight away BirdWatch and other organisations came aboard and said the work had to be done. But there are still people objecting to taking the silt out of the river which is causing the problem now. *IFA President Padraig Walshe.*

It was dry, the air was really crisp and cold and all I could see were the stars above. Red deer were swimming through the car park and the water levels around us were rising like a scene from *Titanic*. Lough Leane was moving towards our doors, and I had 110 guests sleeping upstairs who were oblivious to everything. *Killarney hotelier Niall Huggard.*

This fear is everywhere across the submerged west. The fear that the rain will strike again. The fear that this is permanent. That nature is reconquering the land of Cromwell's refugees. *Fr Tommy Marrinon, Gort, Co. Galway.*

Put it like this—if we don't prepare, then Athlone could be hosting the Volvo Ocean Race instead of Galway next time round. *Flooded Co. Galway farmer Frank Commins.*

We could get him into a boat if he wants to and he could lie down as a sandbag. *Athlone flood victim Adrian Quinn, asked what he would do if the Taoiseach came on a visit.*

Carbon blueprint
Our vision for the island is to have no requirement for carbon fuel of any kind, no need for coal, petrol or diesel so that homes are heated and cars are run on alternative energy. We pay more for coal and more for a gallon of diesel than anywhere in the country ... *Dara Ó Maoildhia, energy community, Inis Mór.*

The dung thing

They are not nappies. They are canvas attachments to the frame of the cart. They are going to have to face reality here. The national park is the people's park and it's a national tourist asset. *Killarney councillor Brendan Cronin berates the town's jarveys on their reluctance to adopt sanitary protection.*

STATE OF THE NATION

Ireland has been the role model for many countries in Europe and countries had tried to learn from Ireland ... Somehow so many people failed to see that the foundation of that growth was based on bubbles and excesses financed by credit. It was quite a shock for many and for me. *Professor Paul de Grauwe, Leuven, Belgium.*

Cause for conCern

Ireland is the land of saints and scholars but this is outdated now; we need to be into science and technology—I firmly believe that if a small country like Ireland wants to compete economically the only way is by scientific and technical excellence. And the problem for me is that Ireland is not now and never has been a member state of CERN. *Steve Myers, director, CERN (home of the Large Hadron Collider).*

Puss in cahoots

I can't understand people who are always bitching, saying, 'It's the government's fault, it's the doctor's fault, it's the cat's fault.' It's everybody's fault but their own. I don't know why they wouldn't go out and dig the garden or grow bluebells or do something useful! *Former Taoiseach Bertie Ahern.*

Gloom and doom

It's nip and tuck everywhere, including walking around the Áras turning off lights. *President Mary McAleese.*

Order of business

What came first: stinking, polluted politics or bloody awful violence? *PUP (Progressive Unionist Party) leader Dawn Purvis.*

Hail and farewell

During the good times it was grand but we can't afford the current situation unless the EU is willing to step in and pay for non-nationals. I'm calling for anybody who is living in the State and who can't afford to pay for themselves to be deported after three months. *Mayor of Limerick Kevin Kiely.*

SOCIAL & PERSONAL

As a young girl I was very conscious of the distinctions between those who were better off than others. I was really conscious of poor people, and that's what I wanted to do with my life. You couldn't do social sciences. Social workers didn't exist. The professions that existed were nursing and teaching, but I wanted something more. Then, when I heard about the Sisters of Charity, that's why I joined them—to work with the poor. If there'd been a course for social work, I mightn't have been a nun. *Sr Stanislaus Kennedy.*

Errin' Lady

The only person who ever called me Gareth was Margaret Thatcher and it was a mistake that she repeatedly made. She managed to get the word Taoiseach absolutely right but she always stumbled on my first name. I am Irish, not Welsh. It seems odd that the Ulster Museum would then make that mistake, because I would assume it is reasonably well known that I was Prime Minister. *Dr Garret FitzGerald on finding himself a victim of the Troubles exhibit.*

In memoriam

When I was a teenager he was an icon to me, a real celebrity. Now I realise he was one of a kind, a showman, entrepreneur, pioneer and, above all, a risk-taker. There are not too many of those around today, and I doubt we'll see his kind again. *Maurice Pratt, former public face of Quinnsworth, on the death this month of Pat Quinn, founder of the supermarket chain.*

Urination once again

The idea is that two wardens would be taken on for a pilot project for six months working from Thursday to Monday. They would have radio or phone contact with the local Gardaí, and if they identify someone urinating, they would make contact, and the Gardaí could arrive on the scene. *Ennis, Co. Clare, councillor Paul O'Shea in the wake of the installation by Ennis businessman John O'Connor of an electrified fence in front of his shop to attempt to stem the flow.*

We can't even afford gardaí in Ennis, not to mind urine wardens. The problem is down to bad manners and ignorance. *Jim O'Dowd, O'Dowd's Convenience Store.*

I would be curious to know how Clare County Council would train potential urine wardens to force the offending youths of Ennis to pull up their zips and walk away on a Saturday night. *Local resident Elaine Kerrigan.*

Hitting the fan
If you and I are best friends, we wouldn't need to be in daily contact to remain so. However, if the connection is based on you being a fan of my book, record, film or TV show, I might as a celebrity need constant reassurance that you still feel the same. Something like Twitter can offer celebrities that reassurance of feeling connected to literally thousands of people without having to do much work. *Psychologist Patrick Ryan, University of Limerick.*

Lies of the land
On the face of it, the fact that seven out of ten drivers in Clare are prepared to lie is extremely serious. In such hot spots, including Laois, Meath, Carlow and Cavan, there appears to be a culture of dishonesty. Put simply, the majority of drivers in these counties are prepared to lie to get cheaper insurance. *Mike Mathews, Setanta Insurance.*

BRICKS & MORTAR

This strikes me as the last yelp of the Celtic Tiger as it struggles into Namaland. *Dublin city councillor Dermot Lacey on developer Seán Dunne's revised plans for his Ballsbridge, Dublin, site.*

Easterly rising
The sudden awareness that there was a potential city to the east of the Custom House and kept separate by the elevated railway line at Butt Bridge

enabled Dublin to create almost a new city, similar to expansions that occurred throughout Europe over the past half century. *Architect Bryan Roe.*

But the Docklands were 'prefigured' in the 18th-century city plan. Both quays, as far as the bay, were in place from the mid-18th century onwards. So, in the overall strategic sense, the infilling and construction of the Docklands can be seen as the last piece of the 18th-century plan rather than a totally new departure. *Architect Niall McCullough.*

Anti-social housing

The big question you would have to ask is, 'Why did the developers get planning for all of these houses that were never needed?' It beggars belief that you have developments built where there is no infrastructure to support them, no lighting, not even footpaths—if you were to give a house here away for free now, I don't think anyone would take it. *Longford councillor Mark Casey.*

Bridge too far

The simple matter of naming the pedestrian bridge in Ballina, which has been turned into an epic drama over the past couple of months, is a ploy by Fianna Fáil to block the naming of the bridge after former President Mary Robinson. *Ballina, Co. Mayo, councillor Michelle Mulhern.*

ARTS & PARTS

I wouldn't tell you that. I'd have to shoot you if I did. *Michael Ryan, director, asked the value of the contents of the Chester Beatty Library, Dublin.*

Breakfast role

People wake up to us, and we're part of the fabric of their lives. We're just not used to seeing them. Morning Ireland *presenter Cathal Mac Coille on a broadcast in front of a studio audience to mark the programme's twenty-fifth anniversary.*

I want to put a face to the names I listen to every morning. Today is a little bit of history. *Audience member Peter Heffernan.*

When I wake up, I hate it. But once I'm in here, I love it. *Presenter Áine Lawlor.*

Cast for the part

I would have thought that after last week [Thierry] Henry was the one who should have his hands put in cement and stuck to his arse. *Producer Fred O'Donovan, responsible for rescuing Dublin's Gaiety Theatre from demolition in 1977, gets his handprints cast in bronze at the Gaiety Plaza.*

On behan Brendan

I was asked to do *Borstal Boy* and that went on for ever. But the first time was about three years after Behan had died, and Tomás Mac Anna asked me to play Brendan, who I happen to have known very well. I used to drink with him and so on and it was strange playing him because I have known him so well. I mean, I knew him well enough that an impersonation was no problem, but it was a strange thing, too, and on the first night his widow left during the interval and didn't come back. Everyone thought she was offended but no, it was just too real. *Actor Niall Tóibín.*

Not their type

Letterpress was the principal method of printing for five centuries and suddenly we have a generation of people out there, young people, who have no idea what it's about and how much skill went into it. Because it's so easy now to do things on computer. People come in here to the museum and they think everything here dates back to the Middle Ages, but, in fact, it was all working in my lifetime! *Conrad Devlin, National Print Museum, Dublin.*

Funny ha ha

People laugh at things that aren't necessarily jokes. They just laugh because it's a social mechanism. In telling a joke you are just aping that. And onstage is the best feeling in the world where you sufficiently telegraph the jokes so that the audience are having it unreel in their own head and you know they are ahead of you. *Comedian Dara Ó Briain.*

Soap springs eternal

I spent 11 years in everybody's living room as George, so that will always be there. And it was lovely, because George was terribly popular. The character was so beautifully written that everybody loved George, which was really nice, because I got a lot of free drinks out of it. *Actor Alan Stanford, recalling his role in RTÉ's TV serial 'Glenroe'.*

PARTY LINES

In the imperfect world we inhabit ... it seems to me entirely possible to celebrate the peace that all sides have accomplished while resisting the idea that we can or even need agree why we came into conflict in the first place. *DUP leader Peter Robinson.*

Peter: the painter!

It's time for Peter Robinson to face reality: his coalition with IRA/Sinn Féin has failed and will not work. Sinn Féin has more than proved itself unfit for government; yet Peter clings desperately to this sinking ship. It's time he recovered some dignity and cut Sinn Féin adrift. *Jim Allister, Traditional Unionist Voice.*

Modesty forbids ...

I have lost nothing. It is the electorate who have lost a man of great ability. *Lottery millionaire J.J. McCabe on failing for the fifth time to win a seat on Clare County Council.*

The Fianna Fáil women are formidable women in the image of Gráinne Mhaol. I put myself in that league. *Senator Mary White.*

Taken as red

Fianna Fáil has a long tradition of denouncing as a communist anyone who crosses its path. Everybody—Jim Larkin, Noël Browne, Mary Robinson, and I won't be the last. *Labour Party leader Eamon Gilmore.*

Stringing them along

It was stunning. [Brian] Lenihan was a pure *tour de force*. One debate in particular was a work of art. Party loyalties were shelved in what was a marvellous feat of reason, relieved by some great comic exchanges. He played the senators like violins ... He really is a pantomime dame. He's Twink. I think Norris has found a new love. *Senator Eoghan Harris.*

'ATIN' & DRINKIN'

I couldn't care less about 'The X Factor' but it's taken a chunk of my business. The fact that people are staying in to watch the show means they are going out two hours later on a Saturday night. We're calling it 'The Exit Factor'. *Dublin pub owner Bernard Molloy.*

Acid test

I started in the Skylon Hotel. The barman said, 'That fucker won't last a month.' He showed me how to cut a lemon, then handed me four cases of them. After the second case I rang my father, who was in the middle of a surgery. I told the nurse it was an emergency. I said, 'Dad, get me out of here. This is horrendous.' He told me to stick it out. For the first two years I was miserable, because all my friends were in university and heading off to Cape Cod in the summers, while I was chopping fucking lemons. *Dublin hotel manager Drew Flood.*

Ozified

A musician friend of mine plays in backpacker bars and has seen changes in Irish backpacker behaviour in recent years. He tells me, 'Your country-men are out of control.' He says both Irish men and Irish women are absolutely full to the gills at the shows he plays. *Billy Cantwell, editor,* Irish Echo *(Sydney).*

Growth industry

If I had my way, no cook or chef would be allowed into a restaurant kitchen to cook until they'd spent a year on a farm or in gardens, growing things themselves and producing it. Then I could tell you they wouldn't thump their fists on the table saying, 'I want it now!' because a lot of them don't even know what's in season. *Culinary expert Darina Allen.*

Penalty pints

I don't believe there's anybody out there killing anybody after two pints. *Dublin publican Charlie Chawke on the drink-driving limit debate.*

We might end up with the situation where you don't have to worry about drink-driving because there won't be any pubs left to drive to to get a drink. *Economist Anthony Foley.*

Great gas

Ether was the alcopop of the 1880s, and its use became endemic in Derry and Tyrone due to a decline in the availability of cheap liquor at the time.

Despite being initially introduced into Ireland for its supposed medical benefits, its use as an inexpensive intoxicant quickly became widespread until its consumption became a criminal offence in Northern Ireland in 1923. *Dr Neal Garnham, University of Ulster.*

CRIME & PUNISHMENT

No government can guarantee that in the future there won't be evil people who will do evil things. But the era where evil people could do so under cover of the cloth, facilitated and shielded from the consequences by their authorities, while the lives of children were ruined with such cruelty, is over for good. The bottom line is this: a collar will protect no criminal. *Minister for Justice Dermot Ahern on the consequences of the Murphy Report on clerical sexual abuse in the Dublin diocese.*

There is no good in saying other than the truth. The Church at this stage has no credibility, no standing and no moral authority. The issue is now one of trust, and that is why it will take the rest of my lifetime as a priest to build up that trust again, because the trust and confidence in the Church has been broken on a fundamental level. *Fr Michael Canny, Derry.*

If we had bishops and archbishops who were married, and had children of their own, they would not have moved abusers from parish to parish like they did ... The whole structure of the Church is antiquated; it just doesn't fit in the modern world. *Abuse victim Marie Collins.*

By the neck
I am not totally in favour of it. But it should be revisited. It would have to be for specific offences; if people arm up and go out to rob and decide to take out anyone who gets in their way, they should pay the price. *Former president of the High Court Richard Johnson on the death penalty.*

The death penalty is unlawful in every European Union and every Council of Europe state. If Ireland wished to reintroduce the death penalty, it could do so only at the cost of renouncing its membership of the European Union and the Council of Europe. *Mark Kelly, Irish Council for Civil Liberties.*

Poor law

Jail should be for serious offenders. Sending people to jail because they haven't paid a fine is in stark contrast to the way some of the financial shenanigans in the banking sector have been handled. *Jim O'Keeffe TD.*

AG OBAIR

It is very difficult to dismiss people. You don't enter the field of academia for money, but having said that, you should have some bandwidth and we don't have any. Our best professor gets paid the exact same as our worst professor—neither of whom I will name! *UCD president Hugh Brady.*

Quack remedy

We're sitting ducks. There is no alternative for most of our profession in the private sector. We're stuck. If our jobs are all that good, why did we have to go abroad to get thousands of nurses to prop up the health service? *Nurse Eilish Corcoran.*

Academic exercised

If you look at the contribution Trinity has made in the past number of years, it has moved up the international university rankings from more than 100th place to 43rd. That's been done by everyone working here, from the teachers to the librarians to the guys who lock the gates at night. Now they are looking to cut our pay and further erode staffing levels. *Professor Ciarán Brady.*

Economical with the truth

Economists are a bit like the Catholic church before Vatican II: all the priests speak in Latin and insist that they're the only diffusion mechanism for the message. 'Sure the people don't even understand the language we speak!' That's their attitude. Well. I've always seen myself as more of a Lutheran in that regard. Economics are far too important to be left to academics. *Economist David McWilliams.*

FAITH & MORALS

The average age of priests is growing. We have 46 priests of 80 and only two less than 35. In a very short time we will just have the bare number of priests required to have one active priest for each of our 199 parishes. *Archbishop of Dublin Diarmuid Martin.*

Non serviam

I don't consider myself a militant atheist. What I do have a problem with is where religious organisations exert a lot of influence in social and political life, the fact that my baptism means that I was being counted as a Catholic meant that I was one of those statistics used to maintain that power. I was saying, 'I don't want you guys thinking I'm a member of your club.' *Defector Dave Flynn, Wexford.*

I would prefer that children were not baptised or indoctrinated. I think the whole shift in religious culture is towards people drawing their spiritual ideas from their own subjective experience. We should help young people to grow into that kind of sensibility and that may be the very opposite of training them in a denominational perspective. *Belfast religious affairs broadcaster Malachi O'Doherty.*

The twain shall meet

As long as religious belief exists, and there is every reason to believe it will always exist, a secularist notion that religion and politics should be kept entirely separate is simply unrealistic, even naïve. And naïve beliefs pursued relentlessly, as they often are, lead toward either tyranny or the breakdown of the pluralism that is required for democracy to function. *Former Fine Gael leader and latterly EU ambassador John Bruton.*

Not a word of a lie

You may be put in a position where you have to answer, and there may be circumstances in which you can use an ambiguous expression, realising that the person who you are talking to will accept an untrue version of whatever it may be—permitting that to happen, not willing that it happened. *Cardinal Desmond Connell on the art of mental reservation.*

Knock-on effect

I love all my children unconditionally with my immaculate heart, especially all my priests who are not listening to my call. I ask all my children to pray for my priests. Pray. Pray. Pray. *One of two messages allegedly received from the Blessed Virgin Mary by visionary Keith Henderson.*

It doesn't make sense to me that Our Lady in some way would tell someone, 'I'll see you in Knock on December 5.' My inclination would be, for goodness' sake, keep away from that. *Bishop of Killaloe Willie Walsh.*

HIS & HERS

I don't believe for an instant that the Taoiseach put forward my name simply because I was a woman. *Newly appointed EU Commissioner Máire Geoghegan-Quinn.*

Chest kidding
We're trying not to promote breastfeeding, which sounds a bit weird. We are trying to make breastfeeding just ordinary. If you make it altogether too worthy, you scare people away. *Sue Jameson, Cuidiú, Irish Childbirth Trust.*

Missing links
Women continue to be disadvantaged by the exclusivity afforded by membership and Portmarnock continues to symbolise and legitimise the ongoing gender inequality which exists in our society. *Joanna McMinn, Equality and Rights Alliance, on the Co. Dublin golf club's policy of male-only membership.*

Down with women
In 1990, when Mary Robinson was elected as our first woman president, we were at 37th place in the world classification of women's representation in the single or lower house of national parliaments … but by October of this year, we had fallen to 84th position in the world. *Senator Ivana Bacik.*

I think it's discrimination of another kind. You just have to go out there and do it. There's no other way. *Mary O'Rourke TD on quotas for female parliamentarians.*

Dress reversal
I've become very envious of the male MEPs because all they have to worry about are shirts and a tie. Just at the most frivolous level I have two lots of makeup in two different places now. It's more complex with clothes, also, being a female MEP. *Nessa Childers.*

TEANGA BHEO

Many people—old people especially—are more comfortable dealing with people in their own language and this will give then that comfort. *Kerry*

GAA legend Páidí Ó Sé on the opening of the Gaeltacht's Clinic Cois Abhann.

Ineffable

We would have to edit 20 per cent to 30 per cent of the texts that come in for swearing. The main reason being that we are on in the afternoon so a lot of our listeners would have kids in the car or the home and they do object if they hear bad language. This normally requires turning 'fuck' into 'feck' etc., so it doesn't really change the sense of the text. *'Newstalk' host Seán Moncrieff.*

Toung tide

We tend to say, 'This is the way we teach French or German and therefore this is the way we teach any other language that comes along.' We need to think outside the box in how we introduce students to new languages and in particular Mandarin. *Minister for Foreign Affairs Mícheál Martin.*

HERE & THERE

There was a flurry of activity and four men surrounded me, three behind and one with a gun in front of me. They were quite rough during the abduction. They caught me very roughly and threw me in the pick-up. I caught my side on a spare tyre there when they threw me in. I thought, 'This can't be happening to me, I thought I was safe in my own grounds.' In the boat they assured me they wouldn't kill a priest. *Fr Michael Sinnott, held for ransom in the Philippines.*

Auto biography

I think having experienced three years at a rural boarding school at the end of the bad times in Ireland is integral to how I see the world and my understanding of Irish society. When I'd go back to New York in the summers it was clear that the standard of living there was so much higher than in Ireland. Our house in New York was warmer and everything was cheaper; all the mod cons were there and my mother's car was nicer than everyone's car in Ireland. I had a unique perspective. *Comedian Des Bishop.*

Borderline case

The impact on the Northern Ireland economy is very small. For a large part the shoppers are headed for one of the UK multiples, and the profits go to a corporate head office in the south of England. We do welcome cross-border shoppers, but it's a short-term phenomenon. *Glyn Roberts, Northern Ireland Independent Retail Trade Association.*

We get more customers at the weekends and when people are off and there's a fair few people off today—obviously not all on the picket lines. *Peter Murray, Buttercrane Shopping Centre, Newry, on the day of the public-sector strike south of the border.*

We missed out on so much in past years in terms of cross-border traffic. It's fantastic now to be able to welcome people into Belfast at a time of peace and stability, with new attractions. *Anne McMullan, Belfast Visitor and Convention Bureau.*

One-horse town

I came all the way from Ballybrit to get drowned wet and sold only one animal. I thought the Kerrymen would look after us, but they didn't. *Dealer Frank Dodd at Castleisland Horse Fair.*

NO, MINISTER

I just want to say good morning to the young people who have turned up, and it's lovely to see you here in St Michael's. *Minister for Education Batt O'Keeffe, at St Joseph's National School.*

Only two bishops lifted the phone and asked, 'Are you okay?'

—admits Archbishop Diarmuid Martin on the lack of solidarity over his attempts to deal with the fallout of the Murphy Report into Clerical Sexual Abuse in his Dublin diocese. Among the general populace, however, reaction is not lacking. Clearly the time is out of joint as November floods give way to December ice and snow and, for many, a rare white Christmas.

You see the model of church that we have—it is feudal, it is mediaeval. That is finished. It serves no purpose. *Fr Fergal MacDonagh, curate in Ringsend, Dublin, to where a serial abuser was dispatched by the church authorities.*

Rome truths
The media seem to dictate the changing episcopal response. They seem to be measuring what they can get away with. They seem to misunderstand the earthquake they have set off in society. The Vatican is silent. The papal nuncio is contemptuous. Whatever happens, it is the end of the age of deference. *Former Labour Party leader Pat Rabbitte.*

Consider the discourtesy of it, and the discourtesy of the head of the Vatican, parading around Ireland in his wonderful glitzy clothes, but not replying to letters and not seeing fit to talk to his counterpart ... whoever that is. It is just not good enough. *Mary O'Rourke TD.*

I express my shock and dismay and certainly I understand the anger of the people and the suffering of those who have been abused, so we certainly condemn this ... If there was any mistake from our side we always apologise for this. *Papal Nuncio Archbishop Giuseppe Leanza.*

There is no possibility of combining either the premises or Ambassadorial duties of these two Missions. The Vatican will not accept the accreditation of an ambassador who is also the ambassador to the Italian State. Neither will they accept the accreditation of an Embassy with the same address as the Embassy to the Italian State. *Foreign Minister Mícheál Martin on Ireland's dual Rome representation.*

The truth is that the overwhelming majority of priests in the Roman Catholic Church are good priests. And in their lonely solitude at night they must be drowning in seas of sorrows and in their tears as they realise how day after day, each day, they are bearing the blame that ought to be shouldered by a few, but who have been protected in the past and sometimes even in the present, by some bishops and even by some in the Vatican. *Canon Patrick Comerford, Church of Ireland Theological Institute, Dublin.*

Unmade in heaven

We bless a marriage for ever and ever but there is no blessing for separation or divorce, which is also created by God and that's certainly what I believe. *Singer Nóirín Ní Riain.*

Falling angel

Well, it seems everything connected with religion is coming down these days. *Labour Party TD Michael D. Higgins, hit on the head by a seasonable decoration from the top of the Dáil restaurant Christmas tree.*

TEANGA BHEO

The biggest shower of bastards on the planet, an almighty shower of cunts—may God forgive me. *Fr Tadhg O'Donovan, Co. Cork, following his substantial tax settlement with the Revenue Commissioners.*

Stagg at bay

With all due respect, in the most unparliamentary language, fuck you, Deputy Stagg. Fuck you! *Green Party TD Paul Gogarty.*

I psychologically bought time by saying, 'With all due respect, in the most unparliamentary language', before using expletives. I was trying to say what

I felt in a parliamentary way but I couldn't. It was an emotive outburst. *Deputy Gogarty explains.*

ONLY A GAME

They are fascinated. They can't believe that these white Irish guys are flaking each other with sticks. In games we are physical, shouldering and tackling. They can't get over it. At the end of the game we shake hands and walk in together and that's an aspect of it they don't get. *Lieutenant Stephen Molumphy on the local reaction to the introduction of hurling by Irish UN troops serving at Camp Ciara, Chad.*

Out of hand
Very humbly they have asked, 'Can't we be team number 33 in the World Cup?' *FIFA president Sepp Blatter.*

When he came out with the story about Ireland requesting to be the 33rd team at the World Cup, it was almost as though he was laughing at us. There was definitely a sense of that. It's difficult looking back on what happened in France. In all honesty, I will struggle to ever get over it in my whole life, never mind in just a few weeks. *Ireland goalkeeper Shay Given.*

I've been a player. I've gone to Paris a couple of times and been on the wrong end of decisions. When it comes to the big teams and big business in football, you will find that you do usually get the decisions but forget about that. What we can't accept is how he has presented the case to the media in South Africa. He needs to show some respect. *Assistant coach Liam Brady on FIFA chief Sepp Blatter.*

Ozmosis
They were unbelievably welcoming. It was just like we were Australian, like the rest of the lads. We weren't singled out because we were Irish. We were just guys coming over. They appreciated the sacrifice. Well, I wouldn't call it a sacrifice, but the big step to go over. They knew we had no family over there. They were brilliant even when I was going home and stuff, saying, 'Best of luck with Kerry.' *Footballer David Moran on his Australian Rules trial experience.*

Ace of clubs

This is my club. I definitely couldn't coach another club in the league. I couldn't coach against Leinster. I know it's bad, or maybe it's good. I'm not sure, but I couldn't do it to my club, you know? That's how I feel. *Departing rugby coach Michael Cheika.*

LAW & DISORDER

When we graduated it was a much more innocent world. There were no drugs, very few armed robberies and maybe one or two murder cases a year. It's incredible how it's changed. The young people entering the Gardaí today are used to the change in society from an early age and are well equipped for the challenges that lie ahead. *Sarah O'Sullivan, one of the first women gardaí of 1959.*

Standing orders covering all aspects of Garda management and practices are not publicly accessible. The same applies to the existence and content of Garda policies. For as long as such basic information is kept secret, transparent governance and accountability will remain elusive and the Garda will continue to be one of the most secretive police forces in the Western world. *Professor Dermot Walsh, University of Limerick.*

Out of focus

My thought would be that justice has to be seen to be done—that is my difficulty with the new courts, that those people who get convicted will get a kind of anonymity. It has to be carried out in public. People need to see that if you commit a crime you will be punished and one of the best ways to do that is the photograph. *Photographer Alan Betson on snapping restrictions at Dublin's new Criminal Courts of Justice.*

Cutting the cloth

I don't want a reference from a priest. I have no time for that. *Justice Geoffrey Browne to a defendant in a Tuam, Co. Galway, court.*

CÉAD MÍLE FÁILTE

When I first arrived in Ireland I was held captive by my employers. It was only thanks to two kind Columban priests that I was able to get away from them. On my birthday I asked my employers to bring me to church. They did and I met these priests in the car park. They agreed to help me. By sheer luck, a few weeks later, my employers left me alone in the house and forgot to lock the doors. So I was able to get out. *Engracia Alteza, Sari Food Stores.*

Great great great expectation
This is an historic day. Drink prices are down after the Budget and the American ambassador is coming. Two things I thought would never happen. *Ollie Hayes, Hayes's Bar, Moneygall, Co. Offaly, welcomes an official visit to the putative birthplace of President Barack Obama's great-great-great-granduncle.*

Craic of gold
When I first arrived in Ireland I liked that everyone had fair skin and blue eyes; it was like something from a fairy story to me. Although I did find it very hard to understand the Irish accent. Irish people speak very quickly. *Nanny Delia Acoba.*

DE MORTUIS

I think one of the greatest memories I have of Liam is of walking the streets of Thurles with him at the Fleadh Ceoil in 1965. It was like being with someone who was Jesus Christ and the Playboy of the Western World all rolled into one: half the people wanted to touch the hem of his cloak and the other half wanted to buy him a drink. *Shay Healy. Musician Liam Clancy, last of the Clancy Brothers, died this month.*

A remarkable man, and he was also a truly gifted artist. He had the ability each time he sang a song or said a poem of living it, and enabling the audience to really understand the message, the story, the depth the writer had put into the work. *Liam's manager, David Teevan.*

The great band is together again, the music is fierce, and the crack is mighty. *Fr Conchúr Ó Ceallaigh, PP, an Rinn, Co. Waterford, at Liam Clancy's funeral Mass.*

He was a wonderful person, a public intellectual, and it is, maybe, one of the great losses of our time that people like him are not coming into politics. He had courage, he took all the risks of leaving different careers and occupations and giving it all to the public. *Michael D. Higgins TD on former minister and broadcaster Justin Keating, who died on New Year's Eve.*

He was firm and courageous in his absolute rejection of violence as a means of achieving political ends. With leaders of other Christian traditions his work for reconciliation helped to create the environment and principles upon which a lasting political accommodation was eventually reached. *Cardinal Seán Brady on Cardinal and former primate Cahal Daly, who died on New Year's Eve.*

His Co. Antrim roots, of which he was always proud, gave him a deep understanding of the essential part that Presbyterians have played in the history of our community. *Presbyterian Moderator Dr Stafford Carson on Cahal Daly.*

Jerry had no time for gold rings or high mitres. That was way down his list. He was very much aware that the Irish church was going through a very bad time and it saddened him desperately. He was absolutely disgusted that the abuse was happening—that the most vulnerable were being abused by the most trusted—and totally sickened by the fact that it was covered up. But he knew it was coming down the line. He had talked about it for nearly 10 years. *Friend Michael Woulfe on Fr Jerry Roche, murdered in Kenya.*

A LITTLE LEARNING

We have a situation in my constituency where children cannot get into schools because they do not have the right baptismal cert. Children are being baptised into the Church just to get into a Catholic or Protestant school, and it is all a charade. *Labour Party education spokesperson Ruairí Quinn.*

As you were
The Catholic Church and the Christian tradition has played an outstanding part in the education of all our children through the years. I think we should be maintaining that ethos and that tradition. It is not my intention to lose the outstanding nature of that tradition. *Minister for Education Batt O'Keeffe.*

Swede turn up
I came up through the Christian Brothers' method of schooling, so it was a shock to be standing there in front of up to 25 Swedish pupils with an

unbelievably *laissez-faire* attitude. It was a bonus if they turned up at all or didn't walk out before the end of the English class. The Christian Brothers beat it into us, but you got a good education and you behaved yourself. *Morty McCarthy, former Sultans of Ping member turned teacher.*

MAMMON

I think we are all very conciliatory and understand the situation we've put ourselves in and the country. We're not the only sinners though. I know lots of friends of mine—and maybe I'm in a particular socio-economic group—they wanted their 17th investment property and their second villa in Spain. A lot of the time the banks weren't throwing money down their throat. *Educational Building Society chief executive Fergus Murphy.*

Now you see it ...
It is going to be the last of the very difficult budgets ... We have turned the corner. *Minister for Finance Brian Lenihan.*

Now you don't
This will be first of several tough budgets and a few more tough budgets can be executed, then we will be able to say this thing is over. *Economist Colm McCarthy.*

Same difference
The Taoiseach seems to think that the euro that is taken out of the pocket of families in the Budget later this evening is a different kind of euro to the euro that's paid over to the banks. It's not. It's the same euro. It has a harp on one side and a little picture of Europe on the other side. And this idea that somehow it's a different kind of money is just misleading people. *Labour Party leader Eamon Gilmore.*

Covert view
What they are not reporting in Greece or Ireland is the unrest and the amount of violence because the people's money has been squandered by out-of-control politicians. The people's future has been destroyed by greedy governments, in bed with big business. *Glenn Beck, Fox News.*

Transformation seen

I have been saying this for the last eight to 10 years. A lot of hotels will end up as nursing homes. It will be good for elderly people. Nursing homes are a lot more expensive to stay in than hotels. I can see a lot of people converting their hotels into nursing homes. If I had a hotel out in the sticks I would consider doing that. *Hotelier Tom Moran.*

Pearly tollgates

The success of the East Link made me think that there is a God. *Tom Roche, National Toll Roads.*

PARTY LINES

These are people who are determined to drag us back to the past, people who are determined to have more British soldiers returned to the streets and more death and destruction. We all know from the past history of this process that there have been people previously involved with the IRA who decided they could not accept the new arrangements. I think they made a huge mistake. *Deputy First Minister Martin McGuinness on dissident republicans.*

Scotched

In this tale of two budgets, would the first minister really 'give at least one limb' to have Scotland in Ireland's shoes? In Ireland children have been asked to take their own toilet roll to school as the schools can't afford it. Less than two years ago the first minister said, 'Only one question matters for Scotland: are we capable of matching Ireland's success?' The global banking crisis has shown that the answer is yes—but only if we are part of the United Kingdom. *Scottish Labour Party leader Iain Gray.*

Lady's choice

I have a very simple message for Deputy Gilmore and Lady Shortall. If they were short of people like myself and Deputy Michael Lowry to make up the numbers in the House, they would be damn glad to have us. *Deputy Jackie Healy-Rae on the government's reliance on Independents.*

Stags at bay

Why should we get rid of it to satisfy the Greens ... these lads are too politically correct and need to be roughed up a bit. *Mattie McGrath TD on the proposal to ban stag-hunting.*

HERE & THERE

We want to turn this building into a place that people will identify with Ireland; we want to make this a place to showcase the best of Ireland in Germany. *Ambassador to Germany Dan Mulhall on the 1815 Mendelssohn House, Ireland's new Berlin embassy.*

Frog spawn

People forget that the Brussels bureaucracy was designed by the French almost as a copy of how the administration in Paris works. This has over the years given the French a huge advantage in knowing how to pull the levers of power. And if you look around the Commission you will see that the French have been masters in getting their key people into some of the most powerful posts. *EU Commissioner Charlie McCreevy.*

Pole position

I've been to the North Pole. I drove a dog sled team across the Arctic Circle for charity and while I was there I took the time to meet my postal counterparts from the North Pole. Unfortunately I didn't get to meet Santa because it was March and he was resting, nor did I see Rudolph. But I did meet the polar elves and see other reindeers, though. *Feargal Purcell, Chief Elf, An Post.*

Chips on their shoulders

After the first Lisbon referendum result, I asked a few diplomats for their views. There was initial bafflement at Ireland voting No, and then I got a few derogatory comments about 'those potato-eaters'. But I would have to say that, generally, Ireland is seen in a very positive light. *RTÉ'S EU correspondent Tony Connelly.*

Plenary indulgence

At the end, you saw division taking place on the floor in fairly unseemly scenes, I have to say, and it broke up in a very bad spirit. That is what I am worried about. We could face the prospect now of being derailed. *Minister for the Environment John Gormley on the Copenhagen Climate Change conference.*

Wind of change

If I could afford to buy tumbleweed from America, I would buy it and put it on Main Street to celebrate. *John Doyle, Castledermot, Co. Kildare, on the opening of the 27.5 km motorway bypassing the hitherto congested town.*

AG OBAIR

I think people sometimes think that consultants and doctors generally don't care about their patients, but they do. They really do and I don't think any of us leave a session where we have broken bad news unaffected. It takes something from you every time and I guess I had reached the point where I realised that there was very little left in the tank. *Ireland's first paediatric oncologist, Dr Fin Breatnach, on his early retirement.*

Stalled

Normally this time of year you wouldn't be able to move on this street, I mean you can see. It's obvious people just don't have the money. What's never happened before is that Irish people are starting to haggle over prices, and that's never happened before. It's really unusual because it's just not in our culture. *Veteran Henry Street, Dublin, trader Sadie Grace.*

Charity ...

It is very hard for some to come to us ... Yesterday I had a phone call from down the country—a house where both parents had lost their jobs and asking for help, saying they just couldn't go to the local Vincent de Paul. My heart goes out to people. *Rose McGowan, Dublin St Vincent de Paul Society.*

... begins at home

If I have to sell my own house—and I mean that—I will put it on the line because we cannot turn our backs on these children and I know we won't. *Adi Roche on the importance of continuing support for the Chernobyl Children's Project.*

CALLS OF NATURE

We only got married in August, and all our wedding presents are in that house. My wedding dress. Everything. I know it's only stuff, and we're lucky it's only stuff, and we're lucky nobody is hurt, but it's still not easy: it's *our* stuff. *Sallins, Co. Kildare, flood victim Rebecca Finnerty.*

A lot of people in the area would indicate, and rightly so, that when there was a pitch and putt course there—even if you were travelling along in the train—you'd see the bloody thing was flooded. It was quite true that it was always flooded. *Kildare councillor Seamie Moore.*

One of the issues that international research on the impact of natural disasters shows is that people will have a complete loss of confidence and a feeling that there is no normality. This is hitting people early in the winter in an unprecedented year of swine flu, recession, job losses or income reduction. To lose a home to flooding on top of that is an enormous challenge to cope with. *Health Service Executive psychologist Claire Gormley.*

I think when you find yourself wading in water up to your thighs, trying to save stuff, you find it difficult to think of being emotionally and physically secure in your house again. *Loughrea, Co. Galway, flood victim Dora Callanan.*

Sliding scale

We have had the equivalent of a slow-burning major incident. We have had over 55 people admitted with orthopaedic injuries following slips on the ice. This is roughly the equivalent of two weeks of regular trauma work in this hospital. It is quite extraordinary and people really need to be very careful. Anybody that is in any way unsteady on their feet should just not be outside in this weather. Please, please do not go out walking! *Professor Stephen Cusack, Cork University Hospital.*

Ass holes

They get a special meal which has hay and oats, apples and the special treat they all love, Polo mints. I have no idea where they developed the taste for mints but they love them. Perhaps it's the crunch but I have yet to meet a donkey that does not like Polo mints. *Paddy Barrett, Donkey Sanctuary Ireland, on his guests' Christmas dinner.*

SOCIAL & PERSONAL

It was physical, it was psychological, it was emotional and it was sexual. *Sinn Féin leader Gerry Adams on his father's abuse of family members.*

Too much too soon

I think it's a terrible intrusion into Brian and his family's privacy and especially at Christmas. The man has young, teenage children; it's certainly not a departure in the media that I would welcome. *Labour Party TD Joan Burton on TV3's disclosure that Minister for Finance Brian Lenihan is afflicted with cancer.*

We're all appalled. I cannot overstate, we are appalled at the manner in which the story was broken. Public people are public people but people are entitled to be sick in private. *Minister for Social and Family Affairs Mary Hanafin.*

TV3 handled the matter with sensitivity and compassion. We had the story on Christmas Eve and we decided to hold it for two days to enable him to inform members of his family. We believe this to be a story of national importance. *Andrew Hanlon, TV3 director of news.*

Sampathy

I can see the tears in his eyes now—he probably wouldn't have turned up to the opening but I think he would be very, very overcome by emotion. *Samuel Beckett's niece Caroline Murphy at the inauguration of the Beckett Bridge over Dublin's River Liffey.*

... on both your spouses

The one thing that is very interesting about being a mother is you learn for the first time in your life what loving is all about. It doesn't matter what your child does. It is your child and you will defend it to the death. I wouldn't do that for either of my husbands. *Novelist Jennifer Johnston.*

Santysized

I can't understate the importance of a good quality uniform, clean, washed suits, full flowing beards, hats and the customary glasses. If you find the glasses fogging up, a good trick is to take the glass out or use a demisting wipe every so often. *Santa instructor Andrew Joy.*

Potty politics

I remember one time this mother came in and she said that her son wouldn't use his potty and she asked Santa to have a word with him, so I did. He was a little fella about three or four years old. And I said to him that someone had told Santa he wouldn't go to the toilet in his potty for mammy. I said that he had to be very good or Santa wouldn't come to him. Anyway. the mother came back a week later. She stuck her head through the curtain and asked if she could have a word. She told me that whatever I had said to him the week before had worked. *Dublin Santa Frank Walpole.*

Ho ho ho ho *ho ho ho* ...

This year, I think it's better if Santa asks for a glass of milk. I mean, if he was to have a glass of Guinness in every house, he'd be way over the limit. Co. *Kerry Santa Brendan Sullivan.*

Winter punterland

People get very into the Christmas spirit ... They like the idea of waking up to a white Christmas and getting a few euro in their pocket as a bonus. *Leon Blanche, Boylesport bookmakers, on Yuletide gamblers.*

Getting their kicks

I don't think men are very concerned about Christmas. All they want is peace and goodwill and something to do with sport. *Designer Paul Costello.*

'ATIN' & DRINKIN'

They talk all about Dublin in the rare oul' times but that's all very well. I remember one time in Dublin it was a case of drink up and shut up: in other words, if you went to sing a song, you were told, 'No singing allowed in here.' If you took out a musical instrument, they called the Guards. *Barney McKenna of The Dubliners.*

Grape expectations

Temperatures have already risen by one degree; if they increase by five, southern Europe will be full of arid steppes and we could see commercial grape production in countries as far afield as Ireland. *Spanish winemaker Miguel Torres.*

Even the worst doomsday predictions talk about a rise of just two degrees. If it were five, we might be able to grow grapes here, but the entire human race would be threatened with extinction. Making wine in Ireland would be the least of our worries. *Co. Dublin winemaker David Llewellyn.*

I have not been able to make wine since the great summer of 2006. I have had to move into apple production and now make calvados, the apple brandy called Eden ... *Co. Cork winemaker Michael O'Callaghan.*

I was in Dublin recently for a wine tasting and a guy took a Cabernet Merlot blend made in Wicklow out of a suitcase. I couldn't believe it, I thought someone was taking the mickey. *Neal McAlinden, Direct Wine Shipments, Belfast.*

No Pope here

Christmas is happening. It's just that they are not spending it on Châteauneuf-du-Pape. It's more normal now. *Michael Ryan, Isaac's restaurant, Cork.*

BRICKS & MORTAR

The Council's policies in Ennistymon are a disaster. In my humble opinion, Clare County Council propose to do more damage to Ennistymon than the Black and Tans did in 1920. *Denis Vaughan, Save Ennistymon Heritage, on the threatened demolition of historic buildings at Blake's Corner.*

Fadó

One of the most positive aspects of it is that it has restored the monument to its rural setting—you can hear the birds sing now, whereas before you wouldn't because of the sounds of the buses and cars. Twenty years ago people were talking about closing it, but now it's not a topic for discussion. *Claire Tuffy, manager, Brú na Bóinne, on the beneficial effects of the Newgrange Visitors' Centre.*

Tara started with a passage tomb known as the Mound of the Hostages and developed over different periods: likewise the Bremore tombs would appear to be the start of Brú na Bóinne. The parallel is clear—no Mound of the Hostages, no Tara; no Bremore, no Newgrange. *Dr Mark Clinton, An*

Taisce, on the threat posed to archaeological sites by the proposal to establish a deep-sea port at Bremore on the Meath-Fingal border.

And I stepped in again

I felt very sad walking along the street today with two small children. I think it shameful to see traffic back into the heart of the city. We had so much hope that we had moved into the 21st century and that we were going to have a civic centre where families could walk with children. *Eddie Lee, Sligo Democracy Group, on the depedestrianisation of O'Connell Street.*

ARTS & PARTS

With 1,000 kids screaming at you, you get an idea what it would be like to be in a boy band. Only of course the kids here are screaming because they think they hate you. *Pantomime dame Brian Dowling.*

It is the festive season and I suppose you could say my life is a bit of a pantomime, so this drama is nothing new to me. *Michael Lowry TD contemplates a one-off guest appearance in 'The Pied Piper' in Thurles, Co. Tipperary.*

Farewell and hail

We ring out the old year first. We do a sequence of 10 bells together and we drop the bells out one at a time. Then we stop at five to 12. At midnight, the heaviest tenor bell rings 12 times and the rest of the bells join in immediately after that. *Ringing master Ian Bell (who else?), Christ Church Cathedral, Dublin.*

Stand and deliver

This only sustains my long-felt theory: in our business, if you can stay upright and reasonably sober they'll give you something in the end. *Veteran broadcaster Terry Wogan, honoured at the British Comedy Awards.*

Say, could that cad be I?

Perhaps, in the end of the day, being successful on telly takes away a bit of your humanity and you become a bit of a caricature. When you see yourself on television you don't really recognise yourself, and I think that's happened to me over the last couple of years. I ended up being a bit more of a caricature than I felt was good. *Departing 'Prime Time' presenter Mark Little.*

Striking a chord

Whether we go to our mammies for Christmas dinner or they come to us—and on Christmas Eve, people all meet up in town or whatever—the ritualistic side of it is very important. And I always think at Christmas, music comes into its own in a way that it doesn't at any other time of year. We do anchor traditions on music, even if it's just singing 'Hark the Herald' at Mass on Christmas morning. *Musician and conductor David Brophy.*

Arklooker

I always looked like a slightly depressed iguana. *Actor David Kelly recalls his role as Rashers Tierney in RTÉ's 1970s' 'Strumpet City'.*

IT TOLLS FOR THEE

Every motorway has an alternative. If you don't want to pay the toll, don't use the motorway. *Minister for Transport Noel Dempsey, opening the M6, the State's first city-to-city (Dublin–Galway) motorway.*

We have a real crisis on our hands. A national crisis.

Banks? Recession? Government? The Church? No, Eamon Timmins, Age Action Ireland, is concerned about the effects of a few centimetres of snow: 'Nobody seems responsible for those people who are not ill but housebound because of their age or those unable to travel to get medicines, food or supplies in the freezing weather. We can't get the Army, their local authority or the HSE to resolve it.' The country is paralysed—or some of it. The expected clichés appear: 'Snap (cold)'; 'plummet'. And, inevitably, 'chaos'.

Here you have minus two and it's a cataclysm. I have an Irish boyfriend, and last week he said we should get in supplies so we don't have to leave the house for the weekend. In Poland, within two hours of a snowfall, surfaces are being cleared of snow. In Ireland, it's what, one, two, three days? Are they serious? They don't do anything on New Year's Day because it's a holiday? *Kasia Wodniak, Polish chaplaincy, Dublin.*

You are too panicky. There's a little bit of snow and you close the schools. Minus 30 degrees, that's when you close the schools. *Polish waitress Agi Lewandowska.*

The abuse we see is unbelievable. We stopped the traffic last week for 10 minutes to allow us to grit the surface and make the roads safe. But people are willing to get out of their cars and walk 25 yards purely to come up and shout at us. I dealt with one woman last week, and the things she was saying were just unrepeatable. *Andrew Doyle, health manager, M50 Concessions.*

Hibernianation

They're like polar bears—they've gone into hibernation. *Shane McEntee TD complaining that the Ministers for Transport and the Environment have been tardy in salting icy roads.*

I don't think I would have been able to prevent the weather from happening, whether I was in the country or not. *Minister for Transport Noel Dempsey defends his temporary absence in Malta.*

You'd have to be thick with the government. They went on holidays when we had the snow there and now people are telling me I should hang a bucket into the canal and get my water from there. Not a chance. *Waterless Cabra, Dublin, resident Eric O'Brien.*

Panza division

It is ludicrous to think of the Army wandering around the country without being requested to do anything, like latter-day Don Quixotes, seeking out damsels in distress, riding MOWAGs instead of horses, and deciding to vanquish dragons whenever they happen to meet them. *Minister for Defence Willie O'Dea on demands for army involvement in dealing with weather emergencies.*

Lough hard!

I happened to go down to check a road in Virginia yesterday and I observed a person pushing a person in a wheelchair on the ice. This is unbelievable. *Senior Cavan County Council engineer Kevin Sexton on the lure of frozen— or not so frozen—lakes.*

HERE & THERE

I've been in Australia for over six months now, and in Sydney for over two. I moved into a place close to Bondi Beach. I needed to get a form signed in the police station but was told by the cop that he was tired of having to deal with drunken Irish idiots, as he called them, and refused to sign the form. *Dubliner Mark Curtin.*

Hair and there

If you have red hair and are Irish, and are travelling abroad—particularly in America—then, begob you're instantly anointed the nearest thing to a leprechaun, the Maid of Erin, the spirit of Ireland, and Kathleen Ní Houlihan all rolled into one. This cliché, I confess, I'm extremely fond of, because I love the idea of representing something so gloriously mythical and intangible that it doesn't actually exist. *Journalist Rosita Boland.*

Never flew ...

I seem to be doing everything in reverse in my life. Most people take a challenge like this when they are young. Here I am, just about 60 years of age, and moving into a new apartment. Washington is a strange place. On Saturdays and Sunday there is hardly a sinner on the road. *RTÉ's displaced correspondent Charlie Bird yearns for home.*

ARTS & PARTS

My father had considerable Alzheimer's but what penetrated the fog was Fiona. I brought her to meet him. She said, 'Eddie, I'm going to marry your son. Isn't he a great fella?' He said, 'Jaysus, I tell ya ... You're welcome to him.' *Author Eamon Delany, son of sculptor Edward.*

Trick recycling

It's getting more and more difficult for magicians to protect the secrecy behind tricks and illusions with the advent of the internet. These days you can type a trick into YouTube and find out how it's done, which is a pity. But magicians are still very secretive people. I'm extremely secretive when it comes to magic, even with my wife. I'd never tell. *Dublin magician Joe Daly.*

Tellyfermot

I remember thinking when I was growing up in Ballyfermot that all the ads on the radio and television were middle-class ads. It was all 'take the car to ... ' and we never had a car, or 'ring this number ... ' and we never had a phone. We had a rented television with a two-bob slot in the back and when it went off the telly would disappear into a white dot. It wasn't quite Frank McCourt territory, but it was a completely working-class world. *'Liveline' presenter Joe Duffy.*

Rising to the occasion

Usually by take three, I'm wondering what's on the lunch menu. You talk about it beforehand, who's going to put what where, and you get on with the physical bit. Then you realise that you have lines to say—there's the bloody dialogue to think about. It's more like stunt work than anything. *Actress Victoria Smurfit on shooting sex scenes.*

A LITTLE LEARNING

Our universities must have the flexibility to differentially reward their best performers, to incentivise those who are willing to take on academic leadership positions, and the flexibility to recruit, reward and terminate contracts that is the norm in the UK and the US. *Former EU Commissioner Peter Sutherland.*

Tink again ...

If it were primary principals who were leading our banks, churches and state agencies, somehow I doubt we would be in the mess we are in now. What if it were the other way around? Think of a primary school with Bertie Ahern as principal, Desmond Connell as the school patron, Rody Molloy chairing the board and Seán Fitzpatrick as treasurer. *Seán Cottrell, Irish Primary Principals' Network.*

Advance booking

The idea of a library is partly about forming a compendium of human knowledge to defeat death and make an attempt at immortality. *Architect Niall McCullough.*

HIS & HERS

Like in a Traveller's culture, right? Before you're married, like, if you're single, you do all the housework. You go out after your housework. No phone. Maybe you would be allowed a phone, but when I'd a phone, my brother used to go through my phone every week, just to see if I was texting boys, and I wasn't allowed on Bebo. Bebo was banned. *Traveller Teresa Ward.*

Black magic
I think Guinness has something in it that makes the fellas want to be with a woman. It makes them amorous and want to put their arms around a woman, so it has its advantages. It's a very Irish thing. I certainly felt Irish people then to be shy, so alcohol tends to relax them. *Co. Clare matchmaker Willie Daly.*

The dolly in the window
On the boys, they've got to have a bulge to fill out a swimsuit. On the women, we don't put anything 'intricate' in ... We do their tits, obviously. *Mannequin maker Kevin Arpino.*

They're just a fantastic selling tool. And because of their different poses, it allows you to put together scenarios, or interactions between them—to make them characters in a little story that passers-by can relate to. They allow us to make that emotional connection. We've had speech bubbles with them; we've added thought bubbles. *Kevin Pender, design director, Arnott's, Dublin.*

Abreast of events
Last night she was reading the news and there was a side shot of her and I thought I could see her boob. It's not that I'm looking for entertainment on the news—well, I am. *Today FM's Ray D'Arcy on RTÉ's Sharon Ní Bheoláin.*

Dwarfed
That's what happens to an actress. Once you excited men; now you shrivel them. You start off as Cinderella and you end up as the stepmother in 'Snow White'. *Actress Dervla Kirwan.*

TEANGA BHEO

The strange thing about Irish-speakers in Ireland is that many of them never speak Irish and of those that do, only a few speak it with any regularity. However, we found that they have a considerable advantage in the labour market. *Professor Vani K. Borooah, University of Ulster.*

Tongue twisted

People say Ulster Scots sounds like a Ballymena accent. But what's wrong with a Ballymena accent? *Irish-language activist Deaglán Ó Mocháin.*

There's no doubt that Scots is a language ... and that Ulster Scots is Scots. *Dónall Ó Riagáin, former head of the European Bureau for Lesser-Used Languages.*

CALLS OF NATURE

It's almost the perfect storm; we have had everything from a global downturn to floods and snow. All we need now is a plague of locusts. *Mark Fielding, Irish Small and Medium Enterprises (ISME).*

Pole leaves perch

Her most common phrase would be 'chodź tu'. This means 'come here', but that is also the one English term she understands, so if anyone thinks they see her, they should call it out. *Adam Swiateck, Limerick, describes Paula, his missing Polish-speaking parrot.*

Compleat anglers

Everything revolves around fishing. I have a very good husband and two beautiful children, but if you took the fishing away from me I would prefer not to be on this Earth. *Glenda Powell, Blackwater Fishing Lodge, Co. Down.*

So far we have found that Irish fishermen have potentially unique knowledge, not only of ecological conditions, but also of the social and economic environment in which they live. They also have many ideas that could shape marine policy and management. *Research student Edward Hind, NUI Galway.*

One after anudder

It's a machine and it works all the time. We have 120 cows and whenever each cow feels they need to be milked, they go to the machine. The cows are under no pressure. Our milk production is up about 15 per cent since we had it installed 10 months ago. *Robotic Co. Antrim farmer Adrian Jameson.*

STATE OF THE NATION

We have achieved a state of learned helplessness which is our response to any personal setback. We simply cannot accept that random bad stuff just happens. *Communications expert Terry Prone.*

Tír na nÓg

I am very conscious of the extreme negative impact that youth unemployment and forced emigration has on family life, the local communities left behind and the country as a whole, which can take a generation to arrest. It should be a priority at national level to develop plans and initiatives that can stem this draining of the future lifeblood of our economy and our society. *Businessman Seán Quinn.*

Country and eastern

Being boring and European means living in cities and becoming much more urbanised. Irish people who aspire to living in the countryside and working in the city will have to realise that won't work any more, not least because of environmental pressures. We're likely to see a demand for, and hopefully the delivery of, good public transport in Dublin, which will make it much more like Munich or Berlin. *ESRI economist John FitzGerald.*

Going to the dogs

Ireland in 2012 will be more of a Celtic cow than a tiger, but I suspect it will also be like a greyhound, straining at the leash to have the lifestyle of the boom times back. We Irish do excess to excess. We're not European in our mentality. We're Anglo-Saxon. *Economist Jim Power.*

Cards on the table

This is not a game of poker. If the institutions are not working and not delivering, then they become pointless and unsustainable. What we are about is fixing the problems and returning to the basis upon which these institutions were established—Good Friday Agreement and St Andrews Agreement. If that is not possible then no self-respecting public representative or political party would want to be part of what would be nothing less than a charade. *Sinn Féin leader Gerry Adams.*

'ATIN' & DRINKIN'

I learn all the time and I make mistakes. But I'm so proud that we can employ 25 people in a small village. People travel from all over the country to come to Blacklion. It's a phenomenal success. I never dreamt it would be so successful. *Co. Cavan restaurateur Neven Maguire.*

Bread and water

I think it is simply not appropriate for councillors to be attending a drinks and dinner reception in the Mansion House when thousands of people in the capital are in real distress because of the water shortages. *Dublin city councillor Mary Fitzpatrick, boycotting the Lord Mayor's dinner.*

Return ticketed

It's an incredibly difficult period in which to be entering the restaurant trade and I have to applaud anyone who tries. It will help, of course, that he is so well known and a lot of people will go to the restaurant out of curiosity. He's always been very good at generating publicity and that's half the battle—it's no good being great at cooking if no one knows about you. *Restaurant critic Paolo Tullio on the re-emergence in Dublin of Conrad Gallagher.*

He is a wholly dislikable creature. He is the clown prince of Irish cooking. I think it's incredibly audacious of him to return to Dublin and expect to be taken seriously when you consider the way he treated people. *Former restaurant critic Trevor White.*

Jarring note

A lot of people come in and say, 'Don't you have a liquor licence?' They find it strange that the Irish can produce something that doesn't involve potatoes or booze. *Cathal Queally, Lily O'Brien's Chocolate Café, New York.*

What is the stars?

I always say that there is only one professional measurement which counts and that is Michelin; they have respect for chefs and restaurants in a way that they don't want to push you in a box, [no] more do they want to dictate the product. They keep it simple—you either have it or you don't. *Chef Martin Kajuiter, Cliff House Hotel, Ardmore, Co. Waterford, winner of a Michelin star.*

CÉAD MÍLE FÁILTE

The greatest thing Ireland has going for it is its people and hospitality. You cannot bottle it, or put it on a computer. If you get 60 tourism professionals into a city and pull journalists and travel agents into a room, no other country will impress as well as the Irish with our music, sense of fun, honest handshakes and eyeballing them like they never were before. *John Brennan, Park Hotel, Kenmare, Co. Kerry.*

Au contraire ...

The perception is that Ireland is different for the worse—in people's minds. It's still a lovely country, but there are some things that are unexpectedly different. Modern roads and hotels, it's a changed way of life. I wouldn't blame the Irish for wanting that, but from a tourism perspective it's difficult. *Klaus Buehring, travel firm TUI Wolters, Germany.*

SICKNESS & HEALTH

I have to say that I am philosophical about life and I'm a great believer in looking at the positive side of things and I decided I would battle it and deal with it and I don't think, really, it's a matter that requires much elaboration. *Minister for Finance Brian Lenihan confronts his cancer.*

Before I start attacking him, could I wish the Minister for Finance, and indeed all his family, well at this difficult time. *Sinn Féin's Arthur Morgan TD.*

Down and out

When Dad went out to work in the morning it was like he flicked on a switch. He went to work every day on behalf of the family and when he came home, he was exhausted by the exertion of keeping up the mask. Dad would have his tea and be in bed by 6.30 p.m. or 7 p.m. He would often break down and cry, he was so lonely. *Economist Eddie Hobbs on his father's depressive condition.*

I can't eat. I can't sleep. I can't write. I can't read. I can't talk to people. The worst thing is that I feel it will never end. *Author Marian Keyes on her battle with depression.*

Crash course

Running backwards is tougher on your body and that's how it gets you fitter. *Niamh Byrne, Muine Bheag, Co. Carlow, on the findings of her Young Scientist project.*

WHERE WE SPORTED AND PLAYED

Every footballer in the Premier League will more or less finish his career having enough money and be financially happy and pleased but whether they're fulfilled career-wise is different. For players to feel fulfilled, you have to have actual silverware to look back on. That's where your memories are. You keep your medals for ever. *Irish international Richard Dunne.*

Having a ball

After school we'd rush home, do our exercises and then over to the ball alley. Then when the big fellas would come that night, our job would be watching the ball if it went over the wall. Balls were a valuable commodity then; if we wanted to play football we had to make our own. Out of a piece of paper and your mother's nylon stockings. *Former world handball champion Joey Maher.*

Horse of a different colour

We saw a lot of grey horses running yesterday but they were nearly white, they had a bit of age on them. Grey horses are like humans, they start off grey, nearly dark grey, some of them are described as brown or black when they're foals, but when they get to seven or eight they end up as white as a ghost. I don't know if ghosts are white. I haven't seen too many ghosts, but they're usually dressed up in a white sheet, jumping out from behind a door. You never see a ghost in a black sheet, would you? *Racing commentator Ted Walsh.*

Turning a hare

We've traditional preserves where we go, or where the farmer gives you permission to go in and trap the hares. There'd be netmen. They'd go to the gaps in the field, it's very hard to cover the ground because obviously the hare will try and escape and we want him to escape towards the gaps, but some of them are smart out—they'll come back against you. It's always great crack slagging the fella who the hare got back past. *Dublin hurling manager and coursing fan Anthony Daly.*

Now yer goin', mate

I think it's time to cut all ties with the AFL officially and promote our games around the whole globe ... It's not a question of being anti the Australian Rules, they have their organisation, they do what they do, and that's fine, but we in the GAA should be protecting our players. *Tyrone manager Mickey Harte on the poaching of players.*

Off course

Though I won the Irish Open, when I first came out on tour, I missed a few cuts and started thinking, 'Am I supposed to be out here?' *Golfer Shane Lowry.*

SOCIAL & PERSONAL

Let's be honest: there's nobody out there that's squeaky clean and as David said, 'If thou Lord should mark iniquities, who should stand?' ... But people are saddened, they are sad for the Robinson family. Here is a little family, let us forget about the political side. Here is a family ready to break up and that is what you don't want. *Pastor James McConnell, Whitewell Metropolitan Tabernacle, Belfast, on Iris Robinson's extramarital affair and its consequences.*

We could all point the finger. But in my opinion, we should wash our own doorsteps first before we look at anyone else's. *Joan Boyd, Newtownards, Co. Down.*

Well, that's what you get when a woman gets involved! I've no sympathy for any politician, thieving left, right and centre with their expenses. I grew up in the back streets of Belfast, but my mother always made sure that God was in the house. Where is God now? The morals have all gone today. They brought it on themselves. *Ex-soldier David McConnell, Belfast.*

We may squirm, as I did when I heard him place the blame firmly on his wife and emphasise his own forgiveness for her, but if that is the way they want to play it, then so be it. They live in that black-and-white world: you are either good or bad, at fault or blameless. *Rev. Stephen Neill, diocese of Limerick and Killaloe.*

I have, following a meeting with party colleagues and one with the Deputy First Minister, asked the Minister for Enterprise, Arlene Foster MLA, to carry out the functions of the Office of First Minister for a short time. *Peter Robinson.*

Peter hasn't gone away, you know. *Arlene Foster.*

Fun fare

Having a good time used to be something that required you to be in some way active: you went out and did something. You thought up ways to entertain yourself and make yourself feel good. However, now we live in a world where having a good time is something that's supposed to be passive: you sit down, play a games console, you watch a DVD or you take a pill, you smoke something, or you snort something. People don't want to invest in having a good time; they want it to happen to them. *Child protection worker Shane Dunphy.*

And beat him when he sneezes

When I see mothers in supermarkets trying to reason with three-year-olds I want to scream. 'Please put that back, Jason.' You can't reason with a bold three-year-old. You say, 'Put that back or I'll break your neck.' Give them a good clatter. *Twink, entertainer, mother of two.*

MAMMON

When I think of Singapore I think of technology; when I think of Luxembourg I think of funds; when I think of Switzerland, private banking; and the city of London, financial services. But when you think of Ireland you think of property speculation. What we have lost is our image. If you take the logic of that we have to repair our image, and how do you do that? You get out and market your boots off. *Aidan Brady, Citibank Europe.*

Gone by the board

In the old days, the game was about collecting property, now the game is about getting rid of your property, which was what gave me the idea. I made a board game for my friends and it got such a great response that I had to go into production, and we have already sold out the first run, with more in production. *Ruadhán Mac Eoin, creator of 'Namarama'.*

Love of Mike

I think there will be great joy; I think there will be dancing in the street at the idea of O'Leary leaving Ryanair. It will be a nicer, warmer, caring airline with me gone. I think half of our passengers would like to see me dead and buried, actually, and eventually they'll get what they want. Frankly I couldn't care less as long as they fly with us. *Michael O'Leary.*

Tot homines

Everybody seems to have become an economics commentator in Ireland, people who don't know the first thing about economics, public finances or anything else. *Retiring EU Commissioner Charlie McCreevy.*

AG OBAIR

It is hugely problematic for people working here for less than five years who lose their job and must find a new one within six months to obtain a work permit and remain in the country. We are seeing a big increase in the number of former work permit holders at our drop-in centre who have lost their jobs. We are also noticing a huge increase in destitution, with many people afraid to access social welfare in case it affects their long-term residency. *Siobhán O'Donoghue, Migrant Rights Centre.*

Deer departed

It's possible they were involved in working with antlers, making combs and that sort of thing. We have found pieces of chopped and worked antlers. They could then maybe have sold them out on the street in front of the house. *Colm Moriarty, director of an excavation near Church Street on Dublin's north side, which reveals an eleventh-century Viking house and traces of its inhabitants.*

Of human kindness

Everybody has their own place for the milk. Some like it on the right-hand side of the door, others just inside the porch. In one house, I bring the milk around the back and put the paper in the front porch ... You get to know people well at the doorstep. I've been to various removals and funerals. And then you come back and deliver less milk. It's sad. *Rural milkman Tony O'Mahony.*

Diamonds aren't forever

We are a dinosaur. Grafton Street just doesn't attract our type of business any more. Our customers were the discreetly wealthy and they are gone now. *Dublin jeweller Robert Halpin of West's, former watchmakers to Queen Victoria and now closing its doors.*

PARTY LINES

We are not buddies; there are very few buddies in politics. We don't socialise together, we work together—that's it. *Green Party leader John Gormley on coalition partner and Taoiseach Brian Cowen.*

Half-closed doors

It's not being held in secret; it's being held in private. *John Gormley, arís, on the proposed banking inquiry.*

House warning

The second house has always lacked the popular democratic legitimacy associated with the Dáil and for that reason Fine Gael believes that it cannot carry out functions of parliamentary scrutiny efficiently and effectively. *Phil Hogan TD on his party's proposal to abolish the Seanad.*

Sin é

I am extremely concerned that the leadership of Sinn Féin has not come to grips with the fact that we are becoming totally irrelevant in Irish politics. *Tipperary Sinn Féin councillor Séamus Morris.*

Not their province

I would rather have a 'Made in Ulster' deal than something which is brought here and imposed on us, whether a suggestion or a proposal from London or Dublin. *The DUP's Sammy Wilson at the Hillsborough talks.*

Western reproaches

I accept that the Tánaiste is an honest politician and that she is sincere in her views. However, her contribution to this debate was such a collection of guff, prepared by people who do not understand what is happening in the Midwest region. *Michael Noonan TD.*

CHURCH & STATE

I think it is a ludicrous notion that you can sue people for blasphemy. I think it is an absolutely abhorrent idea that religion in and of itself must remain without question and cannot be insulted and cannot be attacked. *Comedian Dara Ó Briain.*

This new law is both silly and dangerous. It is silly because mediaeval religious laws have no place in a modern secular republic, where the criminal law should protect people and not ideas. And it is dangerous because it incentivises religious outrage, and because Islamic states led by Pakistan are already using the wording of this Irish law to promote new blasphemy laws at UN level. *Michael Nugent, Atheist Ireland.*

The twain shall meet
It's actually a very significant event. This wasn't always an ecumenical chapel and, in many ways, this college was a focus of religious division and I'm delighted, not only that we are here today but that we're actually doing something together today, preaching the faith and renewing the church. *Archbishop Diarmuid Martin at a joint ecumenical initiative, blessed by both Dublin archbishops, in the chapel of Trinity College, Dublin.*

Heavenly buddy
I was feeling really fucking sad and depressed and angry about what these people had done with the Church. Not only on behalf of the survivors but on behalf of God. I've always been as passionate about the idea of God as I am about the idea of standing for child-abuse survivors. God is the most misrepresented person in all of this. *Singer Sinéad O'Connor.*

Third-degree Byrnes
You pop your clogs and go to the pearly gates and meet God. What do you think you'll say? *Interviewer Gay Byrne.*

I think he'll be the one who has to do some explaining to me. 'Why did you make us such tormented, complex, mortal, longing, yearning creatures? Why did you do that?' *Interviewee actor Gabriel Byrne.*

BRICKS & MORTAR

Cormac's Chapel was built in the thirteenth century in eight years with stone hauled by hand from a quarry 10 miles away. In one period of the twentieth century there was scaffolding up for 12 years with very little to show for it. I can't remember an occasion since the 1970s when there hasn't been scaffolding on the Rock. *South Tipperary councillor Tom Wood, Cashel.*

Which is exasperating for ...

One failed to provide houses for the working class, but the other is going to provide temporary accommodation for a lot of working-class people, namely in Mountjoy. *Local resident Joe Kelly on the construction of the new Criminal Courts using a public-private partnership agreement, while the PPP to regenerate neighbouring O'Devaney Gardens collapses.*

... a highly susceptible chancellor

The physical infrastructure of many of the primary and secondary schools in Ireland should be a cause for national shame. When I speak of infrastructure I most specifically include every aspect of connectivity along with its hardware and software. Choices were made to spend billions ... on buildings ... which now either lie empty, underused or simply not needed. Had some fraction of the sum been committed to refurbishing the quality of the schools and classrooms the nation would be far better placed to dig itself out of the hole that all that accumulated debt and waste has helped to create. *Lord David Putnam, Skibbereen, Co. Cork, Open University Chancellor.*

Giving up the ghosts

I fear that no one is going to take responsibility for many of these properties so they will just sit there. Who is going to be the first person to move into one of these estates and take a risk on services being developed? A lot of these houses will undoubtedly have to be knocked and their continued existence will keep the housing market in some areas depressed for a very long time. *Professor Rob Kitchin, National Institute of Regional and Spatial Analysis, on the ghost estates abandoned by the Celtic Tiger.*

Q 2 P

One toilet will discourage overdependence. There is nothing in the rule book to say that an aircraft has to have any toilets at all, which might sound strange, but we believe three toilets are excessive. *Ryanair spokesperson Stephen McNamara.*

He threw his toys out of the pram

—says Churchtown, Dublin, resident Michael Fitzpatrick as the formerly inescapable RTÉ economist George Lee discovers that a politician's life is not a happy one. 'For the last nine months', says George, 'I've done my best to have an influence but I have to confess I've had virtually no influence, no input whatsoever, and I feel I'd be completely dishonest to allow myself to carry on like that. So I'm not going to carry on like that. It's over.'

I suppose George Lee is Fine Gael's bidet. None of them know how to use him, but they feel he adds a bit of class. *Minister for Defence Willie O'Dea.*

This won't stop them. No more than journalists tend to switch to the law, they will go on switching to politics. They will bear the George Lee experience in mind and may be more careful—or parties may be more careful about how they approach a journalist. But I think there is still a closeness between the two areas, and the desire 'to do' will always win out. *Journalist Susan O'Keeffe.*

I'm also nominating Olivia Mitchell for an Oscar because Meryl Streep has withdrawn. *Fianna Fáil Senator Terry Leyden on the Fine Gael Senator's crocodile tears at the departure of her erstwhile constituency colleague.*

George Lee has made an eejit of himself. *Former Fine Gael minister Ivan Yates.*

HERE & THERE

If Leixlip was in Kerry we would be a huge tourist attraction. *Leixlip, Co. Kildare, councillor Bernard Caldwell, proposing the renaming of the main street after native son Arthur Guinness.*

Trade roots

You can use those people of Irish roots. My grandmother came from Ireland but that doesn't mean I am going to send a cheque back to Ireland. But if Ireland has something to offer and let's say what Ireland is offering is in a tie with what someone else is offering, then your diaspora might give you a little bit of advantage. *Former Intel chairman Craig Barrett.*

No rain cheque

My coming here was kind of accidental. I was doing post-production on my film *Leo the Last* at Ardmore. It happened to be a good summer and didn't rain much. One day this estate agent showed me this house. I didn't take it very seriously, and the next day I found myself bidding on it in Dublin; it was like an out-of-body experience. *John Boorman, Wicklow resident since 1969.*

Stirring the blood

One big thing that I have noticed is the diversity of nationalities. When I arrived here the French community was the biggest and it was literally a white country. Going back home, the first people you'd meet at the airport were black people or Arabs and now here it's different, and it's a good thing. There was a need to shake that Irish blood a little bit. *French translator and interpreter Marie-Georges Bena.*

Funny peculiar

It's the only place, and I've been in a lot of conflicts, where someone will tell you a joke in the middle of a riot. *Former war correspondent Kate Adie on Belfast.*

Cold comfort

It would be fantastic if one bottle could make it back to be displayed in Ireland to mark the Irish connection but unfortunately I'd think that unlikely. *Séamus Taaffe, co-ordinator, Ernest Shackleton Autumn School, on the five crates of alcohol excavated after a century from under the explorer's Antarctic hut.*

CRIME & PUNISHMENT

You don't go to jail for making mistakes, but you do—and I think you should—go to jail for criminal acts, if they can be proven and if they are criminal acts that entail a jail sentence. So I have no hesitation about that. It's another matter as to whether it's easy to achieve convictions on highly complex matters, which are made highly complex in some cases in order to make convictions difficult to achieve. *Patrick Honohan, governor of the Central Bank, on bringing the bankers to book.*

City limits

Let this be the last. We cannot live in this city with helicopters hovering above to keep peace. We cannot live in this city if people going about their daily business have to have Garda protection. We cannot live in this city if we cannot go into a petrol station to buy petrol, a newspaper, milk or the ubiquitous breakfast roll—maybe bread that would have been delivered by Daniel Treacy. *Fr Paddy Costelloe at the Limerick funeral of the murdered bread delivery man.*

By any other name ...

How can I sentence someone to prison who works for a company called Tender Loving Care and whose name is Mr Happy? *Naas District Court judge Desmond Zaidan. John Happy is fined €750 for a traffic offence.*

GAME SET & MATCH

I don't know if people realise it, but the fact that you can get to games so easily in England and Wales and so on means you have a lot of support, which raises the intensity even for away games. It doesn't really work like that in South Africa, in the Tri-Nations and the Super 14, where you really only have local support. *Ireland forwards coach Gert Smal.*

Turd world

When I was at boarding school at the Ursuline Convent we use to play our rival school in Newtown in Co. Waterford and occasionally stock would wander over the pitch. Between these invasions and the cow turds, it wasn't the best. But I have to say we liked going to Newtown because I was at a convent boarding school and Newtown was a mixed school so it had its compensations. *Former hockey player Mary White TD.*

Raising their game

We've had all kinds in the club, men and women, criminals, Travellers, everyone is welcome, once they behave themselves inside the club. What they do outside the club—I'm not their minder. If a fella came to me and told me he'd done a bit of training in jail, I wouldn't say he's not welcome. I'd say, 'Train away. Behave yourself.' *Tommy Dillon, Southill Powerlifting Club, Limerick.*

One won

Paris was a death bed for many one-cap wonders. A lot of guys went down there. The French were dominant, loud, in your face, and you wanted to make sure you were around afterwards to get some more caps. There was a French flair that you always hoped wouldn't ignite. If it did ignite, then you were in trouble. *Former rugby international Victor Costello.*

Big wheels

The French? They're an unusual race, let's say. When it comes to cycling they think they own the sport. They have this thing that France is cycling, cycling is France. *Pat McQuaid, president, Union Cycliste Internationale.*

To say, now, I could win the Tour, is getting a little carried away. But at the same time there's no point coming into the sport if you think you'll finish last. *Cyclist Nicolas Roche, son of Tour de France winner Stephen.*

I have a monument to myself in Dundrum, but Joe was himself a monument there. *Stephen Roche on the death of Joe (Tansey) Daly, who sold him his first serious racing bike.*

Pot shot

The reality is we play sport and people write about sport. If someone wants to throw stones at you, even for all the wrong reasons, so be it. Professional sportspeople are, by and large, their own biggest critics. I don't think O'Gara has ever been the type to make excuses for a bad day or try and cover anything up. Quite the contrary. But, sometimes, the criticism gets taken to another level. I don't like sarcasm and the scapegoating. *Snooker player Ken Doherty on a scurrilous journalistic attack on the international rugby star.*

God squad

I have been asked to coach the Vatican national side, but I am currently working for Ireland. It would be fantastic, but not for now. When I retire I would like to try it. *National soccer manager Giovanni Trapattoni.*

FADÓ, FADÓ

I used to bring international walking tours to see the Curragh but I stopped. I could read how appalled visitors were in their eyes. All sorts of acts of degradation are going on up there and this is just the latest. You can point fingers at the golfing and racing fraternities as well as the farmers and scramblers. And nothing is done—nobody seems to understand. *UCD's Professor John Feehan on the bulldozing of Bronze Age ridges in Co. Kildare.*

Home in the range

Sheila found it while cleaning the grate. 'What in the name of God is this?' she asked me. I said it looked like half a donkey's mouth-bit, as they were always drawing turf out with donkeys. It was blackened from the fire, but as we looked at it closer and cleaned it up I had a good idea it was a brooch, because it was similar to the ones I had seen in books. *Pat Joe Edgeworth, Ballylongford, Co. Kerry, on his wife's discovery of a 1,400-year-old bronze brooch in the ashes of a turf fire.*

Kilkenny catch

You can just imagine the moment six centuries ago—now frozen in time— when the abbot's belt slipped into the loo and vanished. *Archaeologist Cóilín Ó Drisceoil on a rusting belt buckle discovered at the site of a Cistercian monastery in Kilkenny.*

CALLS OF NATURE

It's an extraordinarily rare thing and it has caused quite a stir. The sighting in Oranmore in Galway is the first record of a Pacific Diver in Ireland and there have been a few seen in Britain in the last year or two. The arrival of the Thayer's gull, which is also a Pacific coastal bird, is also very rare. We're wondering what is happening. *Ornithologist Eric Dempsey.*

Sky news

I thought it was a plane going to crash. It was pure white with the flame at the back of it—nothing like a falling star. *Co. Cavan farmer Barry Murphy observes a meteor.*

Measured response

It's not as big as the one that destroyed the dinosaurs millions of years ago. It's somewhere between the size of a football and a house. *David Moore, Astronomy Ireland, reassures.*

Hopping mad

We have more important things to be spending our money on—fixing the country for a start—rather than going around counting frogs. *Michael Ring TD disapproves of Minister for the Environment John Gormley's €70,000 study of frog distribution.*

SOCIAL & PERSONAL

He seems to have a problem dealing with women in authority, especially those by the name of Mary. *Mary O'Rourke TD on Ryanair's Michael O'Leary.*

Look, Mary is a bit old and a bit mad; she is from Longford/Westmeath so I wouldn't pay much attention to what Mary O'Rourke has ever said. *Westmeath resident Michael O'Leary.*

Running out of esteem

I am lucky that I never had any problems with self-esteem. When we were growing up in Ireland the biggest sin, apart from sex, was vanity. It has always been a source of amazement that anybody came out of my generation in Ireland with any self-esteem whatever, but we did. *Broadcaster Terry Wogan.*

Between a frock and a hard place

Some girls have a little bottle of alcohol between their boobs and boys down the back of their bum. *Donie Bolger, organiser, Wesley disco, Dublin.*

TEANGA BHEO

They went from hearing the Mass in Latin, then English, then finally they had something they could understand and now it's been axed all of a sudden. The argument put forward by the old people is that from 2 p.m. onwards up until 6 p.m., all you have is sport, sport and more sport. Surely you could knock a half-hour off that to give them the Mass in Irish. *Séamus Ó Flaithearta, Inis Mór Community Alert, on the withdrawal of the Raidió na Gaeltachta service.*

Go hither

As well as the language, we look at fine art, traditional costume, how to wear kimonos, what sumo is all about and the subcultures of Japan. Students learn about anime and manga animation, and we watch Japanese films. They find gestures very interesting; the Irish sign for 'come here' is the same as the Japanese for 'go away'. *Cork-based Japanese teacher Mariko Takishita O'Keeffe.*

Gael farce

The DUP boast that through devolution it has stopped delivery on the Irish language is once more exposed as mere fantasy. Is it not the case that the wilting 14, who initially opposed a deal at Hillsborough, were assured there would be nothing for the Irish language? Once again the DUP has been sold a pup. *Jim Allister, Traditional Unionist Voice, on the extra £20 million made available for Irish-language promotion.*

Côte of many colours

Irish people love French for a whole range of reasons. In French we call it a 'Côte d'Amour'. I don't know if there's an English translation. Our older students have houses in France. Our adult students use it in business. Teenagers study it in school. We even have mother and toddler groups coming here to learn French. *Claire Bourgeois, Alliance Française, Dublin.*

1737 agus mar sin de

If this was a case of necessity, it is highly likely … arrangements would have to be made to ensure proceedings were conducted in English but with the assistance of translation facilities. What distinguishes this case is that this is not a case of language of necessity. In essence what the applicant seeks to do is express a preference to go to the courts and conduct the proceedings in the Irish language. *Paul McGuire QC at the appeal of Caoimhín Mac Giolla against the Administration of Justice (Language) Act of 1737, which states that all proceedings in Northern Ireland courts must be conducted in the English language.*

O'D-DAY

Minister Willie O'Dea, good afternoon to you. You really are one hell of a dirty fighter, aren't you? *RTÉ's Seán O'Rourke interviews the Minister on the eve of his resignation over his alleging that Limerick Sinn Féin election candidate Maurice Quinlivan was a brothel-keeper.*

I'm a victim here as well. Everybody's a victim. I'm being accused of something I didn't do, which is perjury, so from that point of view I'm a victim. *Willie O'Dea, later in the same interview.*

I think the Green Party have actually pushed him and have deprived Limerick City of a minister. They should do the right thing now and they should go to the country and they'll be found out for what they are. *Mayor of Limerick, councillor Kevin Kiely.*

It has been a stressful year for me and my family. I think the Minister's resignation finally puts to bed the allegations there were floating around about me. *Maurice Quinlivan.*

Yes, O'Dea was a political execution. He was given a good trial but was tottering around wounded. He needed to be shot in the head. *Paul Gogarty TD.*

At least he was not found in the brothel. *Minister for Justice Dermot Ahern.*

AG OBAIR

As a journalist you are used to getting through stuff fast, whereas politics is endless paper trails. It takes a long time to get around things, to get things moving. It's a very different and very frustrating way of working. The slow pace of getting anything going wrecked my head. *Former RTÉ journalist and senator Kathleen O'Meara.*

Scots wha hae

Why couldn't he have kept those couple of hundred jobs here instead of telling everybody in the country, 'I've given 200 jobs to Scotland'? Now what sort of an Irishman is that? He wanted to kick us in the ass. He basically said, 'Right, so now I'm after giving 200 jobs away and I've 300 more. Do yez want them or don't yez?' *Entrepreneur Bill Cullen on Michael O'Leary's standoff with the Dublin Airport Authority.*

Opportunity beckhams

I object to celebrities sticking their toe in and stepping out again, like Victoria Beckham and Sienna Miller's sister. They'll be here for a couple of seasons and then they're off and we're still around. She should be happy enough living with David Beckham or maybe not, but stop competing with us struggling fashion designers. *Designer Paul Costelloe.*

Clothes hanger

After 25 years unless you still have something to say there is not much point in hanging in there. Every season you have to do better and there is so much talent around that you are really challenging yourself all the time. It's been a long road but the Rochas never take anything for granted. *Fashion designer John Rocha.*

HIS & HERS

You women have good knickers, bad knickers, sexy knickers, weekend knickers, work knickers ... and then you have to have a bra to go along with that. But us lads, we've jocks and jocks, and that's it. *Radio DJ Ray D'Arcy.*

Mine are mostly all-white. I don't have that many coloureds; it depends on how often you wear them. You stuff them in and take them out when you want them. I don't pay particular attention to it. *Mary O'Rourke TD.*

It's when they're trying to get their camera up your skirt. That's just the most disgusting thing a person can do. I don't know how they get away with it. *Singer Una Healy berates the paparazzi.*

Down to earth

I asked the wife for a twin-engine helicopter or the socks that no one ever thinks to buy me for my birthday. *Former Ireland soccer international and manager Mick McCarthy. (He got the socks.)*

Ah, men

I like men. I'm completely unfazed by them. I sometimes think they get a bad name simply for being men and it's not their fault. I had three brothers, so I know something about it. *Theatre director Rachel O'Riordan.*

Big girl's blues

I used to say to her, 'If I had your height and your looks, I would be using them to the hilt.' What woman wouldn't? She wanted to rely purely on her brains. There's two ways to think in politics. Either you go the girlie-girlie route—not quite flirt but you get to know the guys. You make friends and get on with people that way, but Déirdre would never do that. *Former Green Party councillor Caroline Burrell on the resignation of party colleague Déirdre de Búrca.*

Uplifting experience

I go to the bar for a coffee most mornings and every time I visit the loo, the lid and the seat are up and the toilet isn't flushed. It seems that some of the aul' fellas in this place still haven't come to terms with the fact that women frequent the bar now. *Senator Ivana Bacik on conditions in the members' bar.*

ARTS & PARTS

I've always thought that books are a passport to other worlds and they're perfect to help grow children's brains—just add words. *RTÉ presenter Ryan Tubridy.*

Tail spin

I was in the other room talking to a co-producer about our new feature at the time. It was so unlikely, I wasn't watching the TV. Then I heard these screams from the other side of the office. I thought somebody had seen a mouse. *Cartoon Saloon animation studio co-founder Tomm Moore on learning of their Oscar nomination for* The Secret of Kells.

We are all appearing in our own animation cartoon walking a foot above the ground. *Maureen Conway, principal, Ballyfermot College of Further Education, of which the three Oscar nominees are graduates.*

Kiss of life

I remember buying a pair of earrings on O'Connell Bridge and somebody asked me for an autograph during the first series of 'Ballykissangel'. I nearly shit myself I was so excited. Everything was a bouncing board. *Celebrity actor Colin Farrell.*

I was at a party in New York last week when I heard this Dublin accent. It was Colin Farrell. I had never met him before but he looked over and said, 'Jesus, you're in the papers more than me.' It was a very humbling experience. *Oscar nominee Richard Baneham.*

Night of the Round Table

The landscape is perfect for the Arthurian setting. You get a real sense of the Dark Ages in Ireland. *Michael Hirst, scriptwriter for the projected TV series 'Camelot'.*

Jumping to the conclusion

Really bad programmes like 'The Frontline', presented by Pat Kenny, are ones which really degrade politics altogether. You assemble an audience ... you insist that you're going to go from one to the other, not allowing anybody to finish. And then you turn to the camera and say, 'That is all we have time for, I'm afraid.' *Michael D. Higgins TD.*

Power failure

A priestly caste, scribbling by candlelight, cut off from the electric current of the culture. *Novelist Julian Gough on contemporary Irish literary practitioners.*

CÓRAS IOMPAIR

Hearses would travel faster than that. I am incensed ... If you can't improve something, leave it alone. *Dublin city councillor Gerry Breen on the new 30 km/h city-centre speed limit.*

We should be attracting shoppers into our city. Shoppers come in cars and not on bicycles. We have already lost a lot of off-street parking. Just because Dublin decides to implement this doesn't mean we should immediately follow suit. *Donal Healy, Cork Business Association.*

Blacklisted

On some ranks the queuing system is different; you have to ask who is last. Sometimes no one will tell you; no one talks to you. They don't talk to you, but you can hear them saying, 'This is not a rank for blacks.' I don't bother going there any more. *Kenyan Dublin taxi driver Kuria Kaguta.*

Lowering the tone

The Iarnród Éireann plan will see the heritage estate, ironically built for railway workers in the 1840s, turned into Dublin's largest 24-hour-a-day construction site. At its centre there will be a hole the size of a football pitch. *John Beck, Inchicore on Track residents' association, objects to the plans for the DART Underground.*

Us and them

There should be one law for all road users. While a cyclist running a red light is probably not going to kill anyone, it raises tension between drivers and cyclists. The last thing we want on the road is a divisive 'them and us' attitude. *Conor Faughnan, AA Ireland.*

DE MORTUIS

Eugene would have been distinctive for his skills if he was a master puppeteer alone. But his aptitude for comedy, character and drama led him and his family to forge a body of work and give an amount of pleasure that was unique and memorable. *RTÉ Director-General Cathal Goan. Eugene Lambert, creator of 'Wanderly Wagon', died this month.*

He was a practical joker. He pulled off a great joke once that proved how easy it was to get a driver's licence here, because he actually got a driver's licence for his dummy Finnegan, for one Irish pound. *Actor Bill Golding.*

He went abroad and played all over the world, did shows with his puppets and picked up techniques and friendships and contacts with other puppeteers, and he leaves all this behind him for anyone else aspiring to puppetry. There was nobody else here before; he was the one. *Actor Frank Kelly.*

All of us thought we had a normal old granddad who used to live in a flying caravan with its own sweet shop. *Granddaughter Emily Tully.*

PARTY LINES

It's not on headed paper or signed, it's just a government statement. *Fine Gael leader Enda Kenny complains about the status of a government statement on waste management policy.*

Government statements are never signed. *Taoiseach Brian Cowen.*

Many of them are signed. *Enda Kenny.*

The last guy I knew who signed statements was a fella called P. O'Neill. He is not in action at the moment. *An Taoiseach.*

Big ask
We have been saying for about three years that what was required at the conclusion of discussions on policing and justice was community confidence. How would we know if there is community confidence? Well, we go and ask them, the wider community, we go and ask them. *DUP MP Gregory Campbell.*

Out of joint
Is this not, in effect, like putting a vegetarian in charge of the meat industry? *RTÉ's Bryan Dobson queries Minister for the Environment John Gormley on the location of the Poolbeg incinerator in his constituency.*

The crooked straight
He said he wanted 'a new image'. I replied, 'I don't really believe in new images. I believe the job is to clear away false perception, play down weaknesses, heighten strengths and put the real person before the voter and let them decide.' The perception of Haughey at the time was that he was a gun-runner and a crook. I think he wanted to shed that, but I have

never been in the business of image-making. *Lord Tim Bell, co-founder of Saatchi & Saatchi, remembers.*

Opportunity knocked

As President Clinton once said in a different context, when it comes to jobs I am afraid the government never missed an opportunity to miss an opportunity. *Labour Party leader Eamon Gilmore.*

Deputy Gilmore would not fill a good coat hanger. *Minister for Arts, Sport and Tourism Martin Cullen.*

CHURCH & STATE

At a time when the state is starved of cash, where vital services are left unfunded and ordinary families are being made pay even more taxes, the idea that the people that created the need for the Ryan Commission are now going to seek their costs is unbelievable. *Fine Gael leader Enda Kenny on reports that the religious orders are seeking legal costs from the Ryan Commission.*

Wife-stopping

Ireland discriminates against Muslims seeking citizenship by asking them to sign an affidavit. The state should not be interfering in families like this. It is silent on adulterous affairs but the moment you try and do something honourable by bringing a woman into a marriage, even a polygamous marriage, there is an issue. *Liam Egan, Muslim Public Affairs Congress, on restrictions on polygamous marriages.*

Rome truths

We came to Rome in a mood to listen to each other and with the expectation that we would be listened to. I would say that both of those expectations were fulfilled. We listened to each other and, extraordinary as it sounds, we heard stories from each other that we hadn't heard before, a measure of the intensity of the discussion and the openness of it. We were listened to by the Holy Father himself, who is a marvellous listener. *Bishop of Clogher Joseph Duffy on the visit of the hierarchy in the wake of clerical abuse revelations.*

It's unbelievable what we heard today from the pope. This is the man who is in charge of the Catholic Church worldwide and he hadn't even the gumption to say he was sorry for what happened to us. All he's done now is to add salt to the wounds and this is very hurtful. We were expecting something and we got nothing. *Michael O'Brien, Right to Peace group of clerical abuse victims.*

MAMMON

In truth, I don't blame the media altogether for the relative lack of interest in the seamier side of those halcyon days ... Who cared if a minister bathed in asses' milk at taxpayers' expense, if the same taxpayers were also splashing about in their very own milky baths? *Ombudsman and Information Commissioner Emily O'Reilly on journalism in the boomtime.*

Down the banks
I had one Irishwoman's property up for sale in Nice, and we had to reduce the price. She said, 'Do what you can—if I take a hit, so be it—if I didn't have the apartment, I'd have nothing, because I'd have put the money into bank shares.' *Hilary Larkin, Hilary Larkin Properties.*

Tesconomics
This cannot be allowed to happen because it will destroy an important strand of the fabric of Irish society. Irish suppliers cannot be pushed out of the market as part of the Tesco-isation of society. There's a difference between what's not illegal and what's not in the best interests of our society. *Economist Jim Power on the increasing demands for 'hello money' on the part of the supermarket chains.*

STATE OF THE NATION

The reality is that we have a functioning murder machine in south Armagh. It is fairly clear that the army council has prohibited actions such as organised beatings, and it is equally clear the south Armagh Provos don't give a damn. They don't take orders from Dublin and they don't take orders from Gerry Adams in Belfast either. *Dominic Bradley MLA.*

Pint taken?

I question whether you can be Taoiseach and still sit up and have a pint in the local pub. You have to dignify the office. That is what I would have told him, had I been asked. *Broadcaster Gay Byrne.*

Áraswise

I'm an ideas man. And I've contributed ideas. I mean the Metro, for example, was my idea, for the last 25 years. And I skilfully steered it through. And it looks as if even in the recession we might get it. All this Joyce stuff. Bloomsday and all this, that was my brainwave 30 or 40 years ago, and look where it's gone. *Senator David Norris sets out his stall as a presidential hopeful.*

Pipped

The Orange Order has to sit up and take notice that the world is changing all around them, that the North is not an Orange state ... the days of the triumphalist Orange marches through areas where they are not wanted have to be consigned to the history books forever. *Deputy First Minister Martin McGuinness.*

Our politicians haven't negotiated hard enough. Now everyone thinks the Prods are too soft. I don't think there will be any Orange parades now, and in another five years or 10 years we'll be seeing a united Ireland. *Alexander Brown, the Shankill, Belfast.*

Knowing their place

I remember one lady asking me to come to a meeting and I couldn't go because I was doing some late work in the Dáil. She stood back and said to me, 'Charlie, we didn't vote for you to be in the Dáil.' *Charlie O'Connor TD.*

This is a phenomenon of Irish political culture and it won't disappear if you change the electoral system. You could put Irish politicians on the planet Mars and they would still behave in the same way. *UCD Professor David Farrell on the clientist TD.*

I go to funerals of friends and relations but I don't do the funeral circuit. In constituencies like Clare it is an absolute must that you turn up at the opening of an envelope. *Green Party councillor Brian Meaney.*

Lagan behind

Our politicians come from outer space or, in the Ulster vernacular, up the Lagan in a bubble. They should be grateful that they live in this bubble because otherwise they would surely wither in the face of the universal scorn pouring upon their heads. *Novelist David Park.*

I THINK THEREFORE I AM ... I THINK

What I'm going to do now is be myself. *Fine Gael leader Enda Kenny.*

It really shows you who you are worshipping, is it God or is it Mammon?

Br Seán O'Connor of Moyross articulates the dilemma that is confronting the citizens of Limerick as the city's publicans (and, in the view of the religious, its sinners) prepare to seek the legal means to open on Good Friday to provide the libations inseparable from a Munster-Leinster rugby encounter. But 'if you're going against God and making a public stand about it,' chides Br O'Connor, 'then you are serving Mammon over God. I don't care how much money you pull in, it will backfire on you at a spiritual level.'

We are in danger of losing our identity as a country. We should not throw away faith and spirituality as a kneejerk reaction to recent troubles in the church. We should respect older people who served this State well. If the pubs opened on Good Friday these people would be entitled to feel that the country has become a stranger to them. *Fr Adrian Egan, Redemptorist church, Limerick.*

We want to open from 6 p.m. to 12 p.m., when all the religion is over. We want to stay away from the times that the religion is on; we want to give people going to those services some respect as well ... I would never miss Mass. *David Hickey, South's bar.*

MAMMON

The geniuses running the banks are no different to the geniuses who ran us into the ground in the first place. I would sooner lie in the gutter with a pig. *District Court judge John Neilan.*

River bank

Like the rest of the country, my house and pension values have tumbled dramatically in the past two years, but nothing has affected me as deeply as the day in 1968 when a ten-shilling note was blown out of my hand and into the river Lee. It was the last of my Holy Communion money and I was on my way to buy an Action Man—the top-of-the-range one, with the little plastic gun and bayonet and camouflage jacket. *Radio presenter John Creedon.*

Liquid assets

The drinks industry is run by a group of wealthy multinationals who make huge profits from selling a harmful product. Small rural pubs might be suffering but the big producers and retailers are doing fine—and causing lots of harm with the drink they sell. *Professor Joe Barry, Public Health Department, TCD.*

People tend to forget that the pub is among the last bastions of cash transactions. It's the one place you go where you worry about how much cash you have in your pocket. *Gerard O'Neill, Amárach Consulting.*

GOD

I find being a Protestant gives you a type of 'brand premium'—people see you as more honest, honourable and worthy. I'm not saying that's true— but if I can cash in on it, I will! *'Newstalk' presenter and former minister Ivan Yates.*

Compost mentis

I think we just die and we're vegetables, we decompose, that's it. I don't know why it is that mankind has elevated it to this other spiritual life ... I take no heed of any religion. I classify myself as an atheist. I think it's all a load of nonsense. *Actor Mick Lally.*

Conflagration of the Faith

If Christ were here, he would be burning down the Vatican. And I for one would be helping him. *Singer Sinéad O'Connor, following Bishop Brennan's request to the parishioners of the diocese of Ferns to help fund compensation for sexual abuse by local priests.*

It is absolutely disgusting, an insult to the people and an insult to the Catholic Church. All the money they have and the buildings they own, Rome is the place that should pay for it. *Peggy Kenny, Enniscorthy, Co. Wexford.*

Not a prayer?

I think we do need to keep a line between what the State does and what the churches do. We have to think again about the references in our Constitution to a Christian God. We have to think again even in the Oireachtas about having a Christian prayer before we start our day's work. *Minister of State Ciarán Cuffe.*

His mother was seriously ill and he said to me he was very worried about his mother. I said I would understand that, and I said, 'Look, it may be very strange to you but what I do when I am in personal trouble, I go to God Almighty in prayer,' and he said, 'Will you pray with me?' and I said, 'I certainly will.' *Rev. Ian Paisley on a request by his Deputy First Minister Martin McGuinness, 2008.*

Overdrive

Getting worked up about the demarcation between Catholic and Protestant is like getting worked up over different makes of car: you make a choice and once you get in that car it's designed to get you from A to B—religion is a little like that. *Green Party TD Trevor Sargent.*

AG OBAIR

From a mental and physical point of view, unemployment damages you. I haven't gone mad, or anything, but your self-esteem is in the bucket. This is a man who managed a recruitment business. I employed 20 people. I was advising people on what to do when *they* were down on *their* luck. And look at me now. The irony is that if you saw me, you'd think I'm a millionaire. I have my shirts, ties and a few nice coats I picked up over the years. I polish my shoes. If you saw me walking down Grafton Street you'd probably say, 'Hail fellow, well met.' But I have nothing. *Former managing director Niall McAllister.*

Bottom of the barrel

The biggest change in my time, from my point of view, would be the reduction in coopering. From what I know, there's only three Irish coopers left—one in Bushmills, and two here in Midleton. When I first started we had 18 coopers in Cork, and in Dublin there was about 20. So what I'd find difficult at times is that camaraderie that you'd have with the other coopers. It doesn't exist, you know. *Ger Buckley, fifth-generation master-cooper.*

Bottom line

There's a lot of training and learning. A lot of skills. A lot of sore arses, believe me. My mentor had a three-foot steel ruler, which he never hesitated to use across my arse—bending me over an anvil if I did something wrong. You didn't need telling twice, put it that way. *Blacksmith Peter Collins, Co. Clare.*

Banned Gardaí

There were many issues involving women, such as the wearing of trousers and the use of batons, but the big thing for me was going into Special Branch in 1985, which was the last male bastion at the time and where they never had females before. *Superintendent Terry McGinn, Donegal.*

Write-off

The minute I get off the plane in Ireland I feel the life getting sapped out of me again because there's no prospect of getting work. I did my degree in Ireland. I did my masters in Ireland. I'd like to work in Ireland as a journalist. But it's just not realistic and I can't see that changing in the next five years. *French-based journalist Catherine Moore.*

No stone unlearned

Learning the techniques doesn't take long. But it's practice then. You develop what's known as an 'eye' for the stone—so you see a gap, and you remember where the stone was that would fit it. Some people just have it, some people don't and never will. *Bob Wilson, dry-stone waller, Scariff, Co. Clare.*

CRIME & PUNISHMENT

It's the loss of liberty, loss of freedom, removed from their family and loved ones and confined to their cell ... It can be soul-destroying for people. They have a lot of time, and things can play on their minds, and as a consequence of that they can turn into themselves and can become a bit depressed and withdrawn and can cause harm to themselves or even suicide. *Mountjoy chief officer Patrick Gavigan.*

Sail of the century

This could be a memento in your garden. It carried the biggest load of drugs ever landed into Europe—and there's a lot of history attached to it. *Dominic Daly, auctioning the 6-metre ballistic rigid inflatable boat that capsized in Dunlough Bay, Co. Cork, in July 2007. It made €2,000.*

AN tAOS ÓG

We cannot afford to be giving out pensions when people still have the capacity to work. I have no intention of retiring, as I enjoy my work too much. It depends on what work you do whether one should be entitled to get a pension if they continue after 65 years of age. *Former Taoiseach Garret FitzGerald on proposals to extend the retirement age.*

I don't get the pension so I'm not sure if I have a whole lot of reaction to it. The work I do is fulfilling and hopefully it gives some joy and illumination to other people. It never occurred to me that I could or should retire at 65. *Writer Anthony Cronin.*

The age of retirement for teachers is 65, and, to be quite honest, I probably would have worked on. I loved what I was doing—I think that makes a big difference … To be occupied is the thing. There is only so much gardening and fiddling around the house you can do. *Retired teacher Mannix Berry.*

Drape expectations

Retirement? I don't know what that word means. You see, if it wasn't for venetian blinds, it would be curtains for us all! *Visiting veteran clarinettist Acker Bilk.*

Invertisment

There is a big group of people aged 50 to 65 who are being wrongly treated as old by advertisers. You will never see a 55-year-old in an ad for beer, a mobile phone or a car, even though they drink beer, buy iPhones and like nice cars. Some 99 per cent of the marketing briefs target 22 to 35-year-olds. The industry has it upside down. *Gary Brown, BTL DDFH&B ad agency.*

FUN & GAMES

I think it means a huge amount to the players to be able to play in Croke Park. Most of our lads played all the different codes under-age; they'd have played rugby, football, hurling, a bit of soccer. You see final days at Croke Park in September; I'm sure there's none of us growing up without taking a good look at those. *Ireland rugby coach Declan Kidney.*

Turning the tables

There's always the threat of cheating. We have a policy of no mobile phone use and we try to be as strict as we can about it, but it's supposed to be a fun night out. We can't start disqualifying groups when they bothered to come to support the cause after all ... It's easy to spot cheaters when they're getting all the answers right except the ones which are designed to counter the iPhone. We keep our eye on these groups once we identify them. We give them a quiet warning and they tend to behave themselves then. *Dublin table quiz DJ Stephen Hendrick.*

Fast forward

It's more tactical, more physical. Even the breathing is different, as in more difficult, because of the air conditioning. Running indoors also feels like you're running quicker, when actually you're not, if that makes any sense. *Runner Brian Gregan.*

Odd BOD

I remember when he first came into the squad, a little spotty bespeckled guy, a bit geeky, and you thought, 'This guy can't be of any value on a rugby field.' And then there was the first training session and it was 'Wow—this guy is truly extraordinary.' *Rugby commentator Keith Wood on Ireland captain Brian O'Driscoll.*

I gave him his first cap and it was an honour for me to be involved with him with the Lions last year, to see how he's developed. I was incredibly impressed with his leadership and his understanding of the game. *Former Ireland coach Warren Gatland.*

HERE & THERE

There's no big burst for the plane at the moment, and that's because they have no place to go. The door is closed to America. England isn't much better than ourselves. There's talk of Canada and Australia, but the GAA teams here are okay for now. *Mayo TD Michael Ring.*

Sex and the city
We have a situation in Limerick where we have no minister, no bishop, no hurling team, and you can't even hang a Pirelli calendar on your wall. *Michael Noonan TD on a garage owner threatened with closure over the display of a nude calendar.*

Diplomatic initiative
Our embassy may be bigger than the British one, but our security extends to sticking our one key under a plant at the door when we go out. *Kildare journalist Conor Creighton, who established an 'Irish embassy' in Pristina, Kosovo.*

Junk male
There's a really big culture of this back in Finland. I used to live in this apartment, and every year the caretaker would bring in a skip and put it in the backyard. People could bring their old stuff there and also take whatever they wanted; there was this mad couple of days where people brought stuff and it would disappear in a couple of hours. *Teemu Auersalo, founder of Dublin Skip Raiders.*

Cherchez les femmes
Women are invisible in this society. Every time I go onto the street I am struck by the fact that there are no women, and they have no place in any decision-making. It's fascinating because the culture is so different to anything in Ireland. *Orla Fagan, Rapid Response Corps volunteer in Afghanistan.*

Swede talk
It's always a difficult decision, and one that nobody really wants to make ... but we have to adapt and adjust to new circumstances. This should not be seen as a snub ... The paradox is that, in a way, this is an expression of how good relations are between Sweden and Ireland. *Ambassador Claes*

Ljungdahl on the closure of the Swedish embassy in Dublin after more than 60 years.

Shoe-in

I can trace my ancestry on my mother's side. My great-great-great-great-great-grandfather was a boot-maker. This came out when I was running for the presidency. My first thought was, why didn't anyone discover this when I was running for office in Chicago? I would have gotten here sooner. *President Barack O'Bama on his Irish antecedents.*

Rising son

I'm in the diocese of Kerry, but from the village of Cullen, which is near Millstreet on the Cork border. I tried to twin Cullen with Tokyo when I was in Japan last week. *Minister Batt O'Keeffe.*

See no evil

You can march as long as nobody knows you're gay. They're pretty clear about what they're trying to say. *Emmaia Gelman, Irish Queers, on the organisers of New York's St Patrick's Day parade.*

A LITTLE LEARNING

There were 250 or 300 people in the lecture, but I spotted him, a fella of a similar age to myself, sitting at the front, so I went down and sat beside him. We'd come out of a lecture and go for coffee, and I'd say, 'Pat, what in the name of Jesus was he on about?' And Pat would say, 'Well, what did you understand?' And I'd say, 'Well, I understood hello, good morning and welcome, and that's about it.' But then Pat would break it down and give it to me in English, and pennies would start to drop. *Mature student Owen Dinneen, UCC Graduate of the Year.*

As she is wrote

I was hired by a leading Dublin law firm to go through 1,100 job applications for apprenticeships. They asked me to take out any CVs and letters with spelling and grammar errors. I went through them all and I could not find a single one without mistakes. These are people who are supposed to be the top performers in universities. *Human resources consultant Rowan Manahan.*

Grade expectations

The evidence of grade inflation is overwhelming. At second level, the percentage of Leaving Certificate higher grades has soared with no real improvement in learning. The enormous expansion in third-level entrants has resulted in increasingly weaker cohorts ... entering college degrees ... Such grade inflation destroys the credibility of educational institutions and their awards. *Simon Quinn, Network for Irish Educational Standards.*

It is probably fair to say that until about the late 1980s Irish academics were very reluctant either to award first-class degrees or to fail students, and typically results were clustered in the middle of the range. Since then we have become fairer at recognising excellence, and to that extent it has become easier to obtain a high grade. But it does require hard work, and we still award fewer first-class degrees than is the norm in other countries like the UK and the US. *Professor Ferdinand von Prondzynski, president, Dublin City University.*

SICKNESS & HEALTH

Everything has got bigger—the players, the hits, the pressure. And the injuries have got a lot worse too. When I won my first Ireland cap in 1994, the physiology was very different. But even then, you could see the way it was changing ... The medical side is much better than it was, but people like Brian O'Driscoll are putting their bodies through an awful lot and that will take its toll in the years to come. *Niall Woods, chief executive, Irish Rugby Union Players' Association.*

Dead-letter days

People go to their doctor, their doctor refers them to a hospital, and the hospital doesn't even open the letter. And even when they do get the X-rays, the consultant radiologist doesn't even see the X-rays, and there are 14,000 patients whose X-rays have still not been looked at by a consultant radiologist. And where's the Minister for Health? She is on a two-week journey to New Zealand to celebrate St Patrick. *Labour Party leader Eamon Gilmore on the Tallaght hospital scandal.*

My own view is that culpability must lie somewhere; it lies ultimately within the hospital, and any study of the circumstances will have to identify those who made the decisions which resulted in the X-rays not being reviewed and the letters not being opened. *Seán Ó Fearghail TD.*

Disapintment

We felt this style and type of donation was not best suited to us now. Guinness has long stopped promoting the product as medicinal and we want to be in full alignment with our voluntary marketing code. *Diageo spokesperson Gráinne Mackin on the ending of the practice of supplying Guinness to the Irish Blood Transfusion Service.*

I thought they had decided I was getting too old or they'd given me enough black stuff after 20 donations. This won't deter me; my main reason for giving blood is to help people. *Postman David Fitzpatrick, Gorey, Co. Wexford.*

Cold comfort

I was swimming on the west coast of America a couple of years ago and two lifeguards came down to me screaming, 'Get out of the water! It's too cold, you're going to die!' And I said, 'You've obviously never swam in Irish waters. You don't know what cold is. This is like soup!' *Theatre director Peter Sheridan.*

Inconvenience

The smell from the rocks below it from generations of gentlemen was noxious. But it is the end of an era. *Dún Laoghaire-Rathdown councillor Jane Dillon-Byrne on the closure, for alleged health and safety reasons, of the time-honoured urinal at the Forty Foot bathing place in Sandycove, Co. Dublin.*

PARTY LINES

Ulster Unionists believe in the devolution of policing and justice powers. We do not, however, believe in devolving these sensitive powers into an Executive incapable of deciding how to transfer children from primary to post-primary schools. *Party leader Sir Reg Empey.*

Grub street

This morning when I was coming down Thomas Street an admittedly very drunk man shouted at me for five minutes, calling me a maggot. I believe he did so because he saw last night's scenes involving me on television. *Green Party chairman Senator Dan Boyle.*

Arf-hearted

I've always thought it to be a mongrel relationship. Either they should have gone the whole way and become a part of the Conservative Party or nothing. Not this kind of mongrel relationship which has led tragically to the confusion over the last few weeks. *Lord Kilclooney, a.k.a. John Taylor, on the electoral pact between the Ulster Unionists and the British Conservatives.*

Seeing red (or tangerine)

When women TDs enter a room they are looked up and down. People look at your shoes, your clothes, your hair and your make-up, and it is commented upon. The leader of Fine Gael commented upon Mary Coughlan's tangerine-coloured outfit one morning, and that would not have happened to a man. *Fianna Fáil TD Margaret Conlon.*

I will defend my right as a woman to speak! I will not be talked down to by the Ceann Comhairle! I will be recognised by the Ceann Comhairle in the same way as male colleagues are recognised! I wear the colour red these days so that when the Ceann Comhairle looks up he might see me. *Labour Party TD Joan Burton.*

Wear a high-visibility vest! *Mattie McGrath TD.*

Respecter of persons

You're no Seán Lemass. You're no Jack Lynch and you're no John Bruton. You're a Garret FitzGerald ... So enjoy writing your boring articles in the *Irish Times* in a few years' time. *Fine Gael's Leo Varadkar to Taoiseach Brian Cowen.*

You're the Dan Quayle of Fine Gael. *An Taoiseach.*

Last drop

Sure didn't I grow up in a hotel before my father drank us out of it? Isn't that right, daddy? *Mary Hanafin on her suitability for her new role as Minister for Tourism, Culture and Sport.*

CREATURES GREAT & SMALL

They come in helicopters with us, on drugs searches, searches for missing people and a whole variety of different things. Heskey went through 16 weeks of intensive training in the beginning and is now one of the most valued members of the dog unit. He has been all over the country, working on a whole variety of different investigations with us. It is seldom enough you come across a dog like this. *Garda Con O'Donovan. Heskey is the first canine to accept an award for bravery.*

Amplified bass
The Federation of Irish Fishermen is going through hard times because they have fished down virtually every other species. I appeal to anglers to make representations to their councillors, TDs and ministers to ask that the current status of bass remains untouched and that the law be enforced. Fish stocks of Ireland are for the people of Ireland and should not be reserved for the powerful and politically well-connected. *Dr Edward Fahy.*

Person to purrson
They don't do loyalty, they won't stop burglars and they seem to have contempt for humans generally. But now I have a cat, I'm beginning to understand their charms. Mostly it's asleep, and when it's awake it's usually biting me, but in the moments between its being asleep and biting me I think we've got a real connection. *Author Paul Murray.*

Cur tailment
Maureen was tilting and bending; she was not balanced when walking. She found she was being led along by her dogs, and she is supposed to be the one in charge. You need to be calm, keep yourself centred and keep the dog in check at all times. The message I would give to Irish people is that you need to change the way you relate to your dog. The transformation will be amazing. *Canine psychologist Cesar Millan.*

Snails' place
Last year was a phenomenal year for the snail at the course. The damp conditions, along with the management regime in place, were perfect for the snail. There are now more snails at the course than are present in most

countries. *Ecological consultant Dr Evelyn Moorkens on the fortunes of the protected snail* Vertigo angustior *at Doonbeg golf course, Co. Clare.*

Crock Park
This is not reinforcing stereotypes. We can surely move on from what other people outside the country think. The museum has both a comical and a serious element, and there is enough seriousness in Ireland at the moment as it is. *Folklorist Dáithí Ó hÓgáin on the opening of Dublin's National Leprechaun Museum.*

A few years ago we tried to kill the leprechaun, but consumers keep telling us that they want them. *Frank McGee, Dublin Tourism.*

TEANGA BHEO

We must not repeat the Irish mistake. Nowadays, the English language is dominant in Ireland. So if the Russian language would be recognised as a second state language in the Ukraine, in such circumstances the Ukrainian language will be moved to the periphery. That is why I am convinced that Ukraine should have only one state language. *Volodymyr Lytvyn, speaker of the Ukrainian parliament.*

I believe it to be unfair to Gaeltacht and Irish-medium students who are encouraged to study through Irish but are offered no option but a test in English. There are no specific statutory provisions in relation to the use of Irish. This prohibits me from dealing with the matter in an official capacity as Coimisinéir Teanga. *Seán Ó Cuirreáin on the requirements for students sitting the undergraduate admissions assessment for medicine.*

Same difference
You always have the impression when you share a common language that you are more at home than you are. So if you have an Irish name, like I do, and a distant Irish ancestry, like I do, and you speak the same language as the people, and you have worked with Irish writers in the context that I have, then you can get comfortable, you can think you are an insider. But every now and then something slips and you are gently reminded that you are not. *British theatre director Dominic Dromgoole.*

Two too little

You can dip your toe if you want, but I don't see the point in that. This idea of speaking a cúpla focal, each day, I think, is a load of nonsense. If you want to learn the language, people will help you. People will support you. Des Bishop was able to pick it up in less than a year. *Raidió na Gaeltachta presenter Rónán Mac Aodha Bhuí.*

BRICKS & MORTAR

In a sense, we un-built the city by building roads that were not needed. People coming here from Dublin say to us, 'Thank God we didn't have money in the 1960s and 1970s to build roads like that.' Dublin, by comparison, is relatively intact. *Belfast architect Mark Hackett.*

Wholly coast

There's a global trend towards megacities for cultural and other reasons. Belfast to Gorey is a conurbation, and, for future development, a significant chunk will be along the east coast. Instead of fighting about stuff like whether it should be in Limerick or Letterkenny, and losing it to Barcelona, we should be focused on winning it for Ireland. *Google's John Herlihy.*

All his world's a stage

Not bad for an inner-city boy, eh? Not bad for a man who didn't learn joined-up writing till he was 20. *Harry Crosbie on the completion, after eight years, of his Grand Canal Theatre, Dublin.*

Dislocation

If Tallaght was anywhere else in the country, it would have been a city years ago. We already have the population, the hospital and the third-level institution. If we're missing something, someone needs to tell us, clarify what the criteria is [*sic*], and we'll get it. *Peter Byrne, South Dublin Chamber of Commerce.*

ARTS & PARTS

If I wanted to be facetious, I would say at the very outset of this bid, the clue was in the name 'UK City of Culture'. Why on earth would they plump for a city whose elected representatives are divided on whether we should take the accolade if they awarded it? *East Derry MP Gregory Campbell on the proposal by Derry/Londonderry to become the UK's 2013 City of Culture.*

I am deeply disappointed at the decision today by the SDLP in Derry City Council to oppose proceeding with stated council policy to restore the historic name of Derry to this city. *Sinn Féin councillor Kevin Campbell.*

Cause for rejoycing
The coherence has been fully restored in the new edition and results in what can be called the first definitive edition of Joyce's final masterpiece. I think that after 90 years of learning to read *Ulysses* we can now learn to read *Finnegans Wake. Joint editor Danis Rose.*

Limited vision
Jim Culleton, the chair of the Authority, came to me and said, 'We'd like you to partner Michelle Rocca in presenting it.' I said, 'I don't do that kind of stuff.' I always said I wouldn't do anything that might damage my credibility to, say, interview the Taoiseach. He said, 'Don't worry about that, we want to put our best foot forward, this is a one-off.' Little did we know then that we'd win the thing again and again. *Pat Kenny recalls the 1988 Eurovision Song Contest.*

Brought to book
Libel laws prevent my publishing a lot of books I'd like to. There are people we've asked to write books that we're still waiting on. There are also hundreds of topics for which we've never found the right author. We'd have loved to have done Eugene Lambert's autobiography, for example. But that's not going to happen now, which is a shame. *Ivan O'Brien, O'Brien Press.*

You can't improve on the book. You don't have to charge it or plug it in. If you drop it in the bath it won't kill you and you will be able to use it again. But, then again, I am still impressed by the toaster and electric car windows, which leave me open-mouthed in amazement. *Author Charlie Connelly.*

Rising to the occasion
You could be working in an office with somebody, and then one person is plucked upstairs. They're suddenly in a different stratum entirely and, well,

what happens there? I'm interested in that. I've always hated the notion of fame, in a way. But I know that you almost can't have success in the music business unless you have a certain amount of fame. *Singer-songwriter Paul Brady.*

Statue barred

I was unable to get a definitive answer as to who made the decision to remove the Anna Livia. Whenever I brought the question up with officials, they said they supposed it was the City Manager, which was just an excuse. The idea of decommissioning artwork seems odd to me. There's so little art in the city centre compared to other cities. *Sculptor Eamonn O'Doherty on the removal from O'Connell Street, Dublin, of his Anna Livia statue, a.k.a. the Floozie in the Jacuzzi/Bidet Mulligan, etc.*

POT LUCK

It was one of those moments. You had to be there—like the GPO in 1916. *David Stapleton, present at the auction at Durrow, Co. Laois, when a Chinese vase, estimate €50, was knocked down for €100,000.*

'Twas mortifying and a hoot at the same time

—admits finance guru Eddie Hobbs: 'Three car-loads of them arrived at the house on Wednesday morning and robbed me of my personal freedom for the rest of the day.' The cars contained some pals of his who are former Army Rangers and run a security firm. This is the beginning of an elaborate training exercise. 'I had to go into the solicitors Arthur Cox to sign some things and they brought me in through the basement. They'd been checking out the place in advance—it was a very serious training exercise. Then they picked up [financial journalist] Jill Kerby and frogmarched her down to the car to me. She was so discombobulated, she fell going into the restaurant and about five of them jumped on top of her. We were mortified during lunch when they kept staring at us through the window.' His day continued as it began: 'In the evening, I was in Trinity College to address the Russian Society. I had to walk through the campus with about 10 security guards. They even accompanied me to the toilet. Funnily enough, the Russians didn't bat an eyelid.'

CREATURES GREAT & SMALL

We know that cottontop tamarins, a tiny endangered monkey native to South America, were smuggled into Ulster recently, but we haven't been able to find them yet despite exhaustive enquiries. The illegal trade in wildlife is booming in the Republic as the authorities there do not appear to be doing anything about it. *Stephen Philpott, Ulster Society for the Prevention of Cruelty to Animals.*

Been and gone

The varroa parasite has become a much bigger problem now, particularly in Europe and in Ireland. Before it came to Ireland there were bees to be seen everywhere; now the only place you'll find them is with beekeepers. There are now no more wild bees. *Dublin beekeeper Eamon Magee.*

Aoife is ainm dom

It was decided in the early days of the park that we would give our giraffes Irish names, so Aoife joins mum Róisín and dad Tadhg in continuing that tradition. *Willie Duffy, Fota Wildlife Park, Cork.*

In their fancy take flight

The principles on which I base my predictions have been passed down for hundreds of years. Before the tsunami a few years ago, I saw the animals scarpering for the hills. There are always signs. *Postman and weather forecaster Michael Gallagher, Glenties, Co. Donegal.*

'Twas the voice of the lobster

They don't have big soft eyes. So we don't have a conscience about what we're going to do with them. *Journalist Fintan O'Toole, on RTÉ's programme 'Restaurant', casts a cold eye on crustaceans.*

DE MORTUIS

He did all his crosswords on a manual typewriter. Because of problems in Zimbabwe, he would give the crosswords to anyone he could pawn them off to who was travelling to the UK or other parts of Europe, who would then post them to me. He never solved a crossword in his life but he was a genius at compiling crosswords. *Former* Irish Times *editor Lorna Kernan on Derek Crozier, who, under the pen-name 'Crosaire', had compiled crosswords for the paper since 1943 and who died this month, aged 92.*

There's one clue I remember from years back that I've never gotten out of my head. The clue was just a run of letters: aknogoelr. *William Ernest Butler, San Francisco, author of the unofficial Crosaire blog. (The answer: 'look back in anger'.)*

I'd do Crosaire in the bath if I was having a clever day—if I got it out to within about three or four clues—I'd come out of the bath thinking, 'I'm capable of doing my job competently today.' Other days I'd get stuck, and only get about 10 clues in, and I'd feel I couldn't be trusted to do anything serious. *Singer and film-maker Nick Kelly.*

Here for the bier

It was built around the late '50s or early '60s. There was a lot of cross-border smuggling in those days and the coffin had an important secondary role. If the hearse driver was stopped by the Customs he would explain that he was returning with a body from Dublin. They never asked to open it. *Geoffrey Simpson, Viewback Antiques, on a coffin for sale in Ballyshannon, Co. Donegal.*

FUN & GAMES

I'm Irish—I don't even give my brothers hugs! *Golfer Pádraig Harrington on Tiger Woods revealing that he has been hugged by players since returning to the tour.*

Words fail him

This decision could only have been made in a marketing department, by a group of highly qualified 19-year-old morons who have never actually played the game. Remember Breo? The white Guinness? I can only hope that Scrabble with Capital Letters joins it in the graveyard of dodgy ideas from the dudes in marketing. *Scrabble fan Ian Trevor on the admission of proper names and brand names.*

Time, gentlemen

To be honest, I find it mildly embarrassing, all these reunions and functions. I mean, who the hell wants to see all these 70-plus-year-old boys? Increasingly we mean even less because so many people weren't even born back then. There's been a hell of a lot of people buried that were in Croke Park that day in 1960. *Down captain Kevin Mussen, first to bring the Sam Maguire over the border.*

Sore thing

I played in Thomond Park in 1995 and when you go there the intimidation factor is absolutely huge; they do everything to try and put you off your game. *Former rugby international Neil Francis.*

What were you expecting, sandwiches and fizzy drinks? *Setanta interviewer Daire O'Brien.*

No, but they changed the Andrex and put in sandpaper. *Neil Francis.*

Battle of all mothers

Jesus, when I saw their pusses coming through the bit of an old gate to the dressing rooms down there. In fairness, the boys Ritchie and Vinnie and Hedgo had a chat with them in Dublin before they left, but it was Mothers' Day and it was like they were down for their Mothers' Day spin. Like collecting the mother out of the nursing home and bringing her down the country for an old spin. Gentle Jesus! *Dublin hurling bainisteoir Anthony Daly regrets relaxing the training schedule before confronting Offaly.*

Bridge too far

I was working in London when I was a student, so when the season started I went along to Stamford Bridge. It was ugly. It was terrible. It was the late '70s. There was a lot of violence. The atmosphere when you got off the Tube was just awful. I went to quite a few games in '78 and '79 and stayed away then. I didn't like what was going on. *Novelist and restored Chelsea supporter Roddy Doyle.*

Tee ceremony

It's a ceremony. There are lots of lovely things about golf which are nice; they're stupid, but they're nice. There's a civility to it, not that I practise that very much. There's a code of honour—if you make a mistake or play a foul shot and nobody has seen it, you own up to it. *Actor and comedian Niall Tóibín.*

Windsor all right

Everyone knows she's mad about racing, so why not make her first trip to Ireland next week? She can always stay at home for her official birthday in June. And what's more, we'll even ensure the weather is lovely—Fr Breen will look after us on that one. *Punchestown manager Dick O'Sullivan, on being told that Britain's Queen would love to attend the festival but can't because it clashes with her birthday.*

No score

Attempts on goals are like going to a nightclub; you could speak to 50 girls, but if you're going home on your own it's no good, is it? You could only speak to one and go home with her. *Former Ireland captain Roy Keane.*

'ATIN' & DRINKIN'

Welcome to the shimmering alcoholic oasis at the end of the N7. *Limerick PRO Laura Ryan on the occasion of some of the city's pubs being permitted to open for the first time on Good Friday as Munster rugby entertains Leinster.*

We don't have any Setanta, Sky, RTÉ or even TG4 here. This is a pub for stimulating conversation, whether it be about Munster rugby or the economic affairs of Outer Mongolia, and we are benefiting from this decision, so I have no complaints. *White House, Limerick, proprietor Glen McLoughlin.*

Dub with no beer

I don't expect to make much money, but I want to provide a service to people who are discommoded on Good Friday. The laws should be changed. If you want to go to church, that is fine, but you don't spend all day there. *Dublin publican Charlie Chawke, serving food only.*

Go figure

I've no idea how they get the figs into the fig rolls. *Michael Carey, chairman, biscuit-maker Jacob Fruitfield.*

CRIME & PUNISHMENT

There was nothing really to worry about up to Toyosi's death. But we have a sense of being a highly diverse community, one that is not settled, that is going to take a shape or form as it progresses, and rather than allowing it to become the kind of animal that it would become naturally, we want to lead it to become what it should be. *Dare Adetuberu, Pastor of the Redeemed Christian Church of God, Tyrrelstown, Co. Dublin, on the murder of local teenager Toyosi Shittabey.*

He had been living here 11 years. We thought we were safe here. It is not like we went to some mad place where we weren't supposed to go. It has gone too far. *Toyosi's friend Bobby Kuti.*

It is important to remain calm. He was an Irish boy as well as an African boy. There have been racial tensions in Ireland for some time; we have been highlighting them. There have been many violent racial incidents in the past few years. We have to make sure problems do not develop now. *Eric Wao, co-ordinator of the Africa Centre.*

Behind closed doors

There is a sense of, I don't know if it's the right word, embarrassment about how the investigation went, and people really felt for the family because they still have no closure. After it happened people started to look back, and it was worked out that it was the first murder in the area in 100 years. This really was the kind of place where you never locked your door at night, but there was a definite sea-change after that. *Publican Dermot O'Sullivan, Crookhaven, Co. Cork, on the murder of Sophie Toscan du Plantier in 1996.*

Cleared for take-off

Why should we keep him here? We have enough to be doing. A guy like this is no asset, a man that is cultivating drugs. If this was France or Germany, he would be on the next boat or plane out. We are a laughing-stock. The other countries in Europe don't seem to have the same qualms about this. If this was the USA, this fella would not get past the airport. He would not get past the customs. I can't get my head around this case. *Judge Seán MacBride, Cavan District Court, admits to his perplexity.*

AG OBAIR

He said, 'I need you to do a favour for me.' 'Well,' I said, 'you know I'm in Spain. It might be difficult to do a favour for you.' 'Ah, no,' he said, 'not that kind of a favour.' And I said, 'Okay, what's this all about?' And he said, 'Would you go as Irish nominee to the Court of Auditors for six years?'

Máire Geoghegan-Quinn, now EU Commissioner, recalls getting a new job from Taoiseach Bertie Ahern.

Fuel's errand
I get the impression that if these guys could buy turf in Iceland, that's where they'd go, rather than here. *Brian Reilly, Future Print, on the Revenue Commissioners' spending €225,000 to have tax forms printed in Spain.*

Washington post
Charlie had totally different circumstances to me. It is not fair to compare. I was 26. There were no cutbacks. I could get on a plane whenever I wanted. Charlie was older and was being held up to expectations that, from the very beginning, he was going to have difficulty fulfilling. I'd never judge him for it. The one thing I'd disagree with him about is the notion that Washington is a lonely place to be. That is the total opposite of my experience. *RTÉ's Mark Little on his predecessor, Mr Bird.*

It's Charlie Bird from RTÉ ... Why are you ducking down, Mr Drumm? *In leafy Cape Cod, an intrepid reporter knocks on former Anglo Irish Bank executive's front door.*

Unfair cop
He has crossed the line and entered into the political arena and he has clearly breached a fundamental condition of his employment as a member of An Garda Síochána. I mean, for me to hear a member of An Garda Síochána accuse a sovereign government of robbery, corruption and treason, and this coming from a member of An Garda Síochána, who are the agents of the State to investigate and prosecute these types of crimes, it's just clearly not sustainable. *Minister for Justice Dermot Ahern on an undelivered address by Michael O'Boyce, outgoing president of the Garda Representative Association.*

From a height
Essentially it's like you call 999 and the fire brigade pulls their engines out of the backyard and get their helmets out of the attic. *Hugh McLindon, Glen of Imaal Mountain Rescue Team, on being obliged to store their equipment in sitting-rooms and sheds.*

MAMMON

I must apologise for crimes against good taste. *British economist Kevin Gardiner regrets inventing the term 'Celtic Tiger' in 1994.*

All I know is that it is becoming a Celtic Chernobyl. *Economist Peter Bacon on Anglo Irish Bank.*

Quinn's worth

He got too greedy. This is not good for Cavan; he was a great employer and he built up his business from nothing. He got too greedy but I think he'll survive. *Vincent Reilly, Cavan, on the collapse of the Seán Quinn empire.*

We're not short of cash; we're just short of meeting the requirements of the Regulator at the present time. *Seán Quinn.*

I have said all along in discussions with the company, 'Show me the money and we will take a different approach,' but no one has been forthcoming. *Financial Regulator Matthew Elderfield.*

I think Seán Quinn put a gun to the head of the government about things that were going on at the Anglo Irish Bank, and this is their way of backlashing at him. I have a feeling that's it. *Pauric McArdle, Cavan.*

Cudology

Cows don't do low-fat or Supermilk, and someone has to pay for all the milk that goes down the drain because it has gone off in the shops. *Simon Burke, Superquinn, on farmers' criticisms of supermarket margins.*

Bling on the girls

Women can't be seen to be wearing bling-tastic clothes these days and are afraid to show off ostentatious wealth, as they don't want anyone to know, so they are spending as much as they want on expensive underwear, which no one can see. *Susan Hunter, Susan Hunter Lingerie, Dublin.*

TEANGA BHEO

The dictionary is a wonderful book and people should be sent to it regularly. Do you know, when you get up in the morning and you stretch and you yawn, there's a word for it? Not a beautiful word, not one that trips lightly from the pen, but a marvellous word: pandiculation. Isn't that wonderful? So now, when you yawn and stretch, you're pandiculating. *Novelist John Banville.*

Learning the slanguage
I should be allowed to reply without interruption and not have to listen to some of Deputy McCormack's guff. He is the gurrier-in-chief when it comes to that sort of thing. *Taoiseach Brian Cowen.*

He referred to me as a 'gurrier'. I have looked up the Oxford English Dictionary and the Anglo-Irish dictionary and noted there is no explanation for the word. Therefore, it must be an awfully bad word entirely. *Pádraic McCormack TD.*

Decline and fall
It must be acknowledged that compulsion, as the political engine to revive the Irish language, has failed. Forcing students to learn Irish is not working and is actually driving many young people away from any real engagement with this beautiful language. *Brian Hayes TD.*

I am anxious that the approach being taken could have an impact on our objective in the 20-year strategy for the Irish language to have 250,000 speakers—three times the current level—using Irish daily outside of the education system. If we don't set high aims now, it's going to be difficult to achieve that. *Minister for the Gaeltacht Pat Carey on the new 'literature-lite' Leaving Cert syllabus.*

PARTY LINES

I am fully conscious that I am not the unanimous choice of this Assembly, but I do say to every member of this house that we have a duty together to provide leadership, and if we didn't know that before, we sadly had a reminder of it at half past twelve this morning. *Taking office, new NI*

Minister of Justice David Ford reflects on the Holywood, Co. Down, bomb attack by dissident republicans.

Talking Turkey

The reasons for opposing Turkish membership are manifold. The most obvious issue which is of grave concern is the capacity of the European Union to absorb a hugely populated country of 72 million people ... It is also fair to say that from a geographical perspective, Turkey cannot be considered to be a part of Europe. *Fine Gael TD Lucinda Creighton.*

Deputy Creighton should remember that it has been long-standing Irish government policy to support Turkish membership of the European Union, and her attempt to derail this worthwhile inclusion of Turkey by scaremongering on the issue of unemployment is not appropriate. *Fianna Fáil TD Michael Mulcahy.*

Conflict revolution

First of all there was no physical assault of any description on anyone. It was just they exchanged a few pleasantries. Ferris and Fahey met at the revolving door on the way in to Leinster House one morning—it was obvious they didn't like one another. I just said, 'Ye picked a bad place to have a row, lads,' and the whole thing was over in ten or 20 seconds. *Paul Connaughton TD on an alleged pugilistic confrontation between colleagues Martin Ferris and Frank Fahey.*

Green, orange, red

In some UK regions the state accounts for a bigger share of the economy than it did in the communist countries of the old eastern bloc—it is clearly unsustainable. I think the first one I would pick out is Northern Ireland. In Northern Ireland it is quite clear, almost every party, I think, accepts that the size of the state has got too big—we need a bigger private sector. *British Conservative Party leader David Cameron.*

Sleeveens

Cowen is affecting high dudgeon in a way that doesn't convince anybody. Do we forget the queues down in Galway to tug Bertie Ahern's sleeve during the Galway Races by every developer in town and by every big banker? Why?

Because of the legislation that they were getting and the facilitation of the profiteering that was going on. *Joe Higgins MEP.*

SOCIAL & PERSONAL

Are you married? I bet you are. I find people who are married want the rest of us to suffer too. I never got married and I'm 58, so why would I now? *RTÉ newsreader Anne Doyle.*

UFOs

I can neither confirm nor deny the underwear reports because the spotlights were too strong and I wasn't able to identify what was flying about. *Did ladies throw their knickers at Charlie Flanagan TD during his catwalk turn at a charity event?*

Glimmer men

If the Russians turn the gas off for a prolonged period during a bad winter, you're probably talking about hundreds of thousands of people dying in Germany. They would simply freeze to death. In Ireland, the lights would go out and the economy would effectively grind to a halt. *ESRI economist Richard Tol.*

Head cases

I'm far more worried about them than I was about swine flu because anecdotally I'm hearing of two or three patients a week being seen in most emergency departments as a result of taking head-shop products, and the presentations are really scary. *Dr Chris Luke, Cork.*

Cross purposes

We are very angry and very frustrated and don't trust anybody any more. This anger is part of the purging of the past, but the purging is slowed by the fact that we can't get rid of the people who we don't trust. We seem to be stuck with so many of those who caused these problems in the first place. *Carolyn Odgers, Chemistry ad agency, on the results of a survey.*

As you were

There are many people still *in situ* who were tainted by the culture and they will revert to type within a year or two years when things settle down. The next generation of deputies in fifteen or 20 years' time will be back again to discuss another banking crisis. *Former Fine Gael leader Michael Noonan.*

A LITTLE LEARNING

The Christian Brothers were fairly mangled fellows in Navan. Some men speak highly of them. Unfortunately I never saw that. I just remember the brutality. *Actor Pierce Brosnan.*

The horse's mouth
The librarian in Wormwood Scrubs seemed to think I was some kind of reincarnation of Brendan Behan. She was always very helpful when I was looking for books. One day I was wandering around the shelves in the library and came across *UXB* [*unexploded bomb*], written by a British Army bomb disposal expert. It made very interesting and informative reading. *Former IRA bomber Jim 'Mortar' Monaghan.*

No room at the intake
The National Archives has now been full for many years ... We are actually being forced to break the law by not carrying out our statutory duty to preserve and make available government records which are more than 30 years old. The building we occupy is inadequate and lacking in basic educational facilities. *Catriona Crowe, National Archives.*

Drama on Inis
We gather on this one day knowing that it is the culmination of over 10 years of careful planning and pilot projects and that it marks something quite remarkable and wonderful—the successful delivery of a fully accredited degree programme on an island. *President Mary McAleese on Sherkin Island, Co. Cork, for the award of Dublin Institute of Technology degrees.*

No shirkin'
If you really want to do it, it's never too late. A lot of people close their minds when they reach 65. A lot of people have to change their attitude to old age. And if my speaking about it today does that, then I'll be happy. *Peggy Townend (82), recipient of the DIT BA in Visual Art.*

Addaptation

The whole situation was fraught because Haughey did not welcome delays and the boss did not tolerate mistakes. We quickly became numerically proficient in a way that today's school-leavers can only dream of. *Economist Pat McArdle on working in the Department of Finance.*

Shinlanigans

We have been asked to take one step back to take two steps forward. There's not enough room in our overcrowded classrooms to do this little dance. *Bernie Ruane, Teachers' Union of Ireland.*

CLASH OF THE ASH

It's really unfathomable, but nature is nature. There is not a thing you can do about it, to be honest, other than feeling desperately sorry for everyone. We've really had blow after blow in the tourism industry, and this is making things go from bad to worse. *Eamonn McKeon, Irish Tourist Industry Confederation, on the economic fallout from the eruption of the unpronounceable Icelandic volcano, Eyjafjallajökull.*

The hotel decided we were eating too many salads, because we didn't have that many euros left, so they said they would fix us dinner for just €8 every night. I thought, 'Oh! We are so special!' *Doris Hill, North Carolina, stranded in Dublin.*

Some people think we overacted, and of course that's the easy thing for people to say now. If a plane crashed in Irish air space I'm sure I'd be in here in this House trying to explain myself as to why I didn't tell the aviation authority to close down Irish air space. *Minister for Transport Noel Dempsey.*

My difficulty is that they have not published the criteria. In other words, what was the level of the contamination that caused the closure of air space? Our information is that the vast area of Ireland did not have contamination. *Evan Collins, Irish Airline Pilots' Association.*

This has been dreadful for Europe, definitely. But with any safety risk that occurs, the first response must be to stop aircraft flying. *Dubliner Brian Flynn, Eurocontrol.*

Air ash arís

It's mad busy. It hasn't stopped all day. It's amazing what one little volcano can do. *Margaret Hegarty, Fastnet Line, Cork–Swansea ferry service.*

CHURCH & STATE

Your church is not welcome in my country any more! It is a Nazi religion. I want it to leave my country. I want you to leave my country. *Abuse victim John Ayers to Archbishop Diarmuid Martin on the steps of the Pro-Cathedral in Dublin.*

Canterbury lam

I was speaking to an Irish friend recently who was saying that it's quite difficult in some parts of Ireland to go down the street wearing a clerical collar now. And an institution so deeply bound into the life of a society suddenly becoming, suddenly losing all credibility—that's not a problem for the church, it's a problem for everybody in Ireland. *Archbishop of Canterbury Rowan Williams.*

The remarks of the Archbishop of Canterbury, over which admittedly he has now expressed regret, which described the Roman Catholic Church in Ireland as having lost all credibility, were not helpful. The lay people of the Roman Catholic Church do not deserve to be criticised for the failings of some of their bishops and priests. *Archbishop of Armagh Alan Harper.*

Speaking frankly, I have to say that in all my years as Archbishop of Dublin, in difficult times, I have rarely felt personally so discouraged as this morning when I woke to hear Archbishop Williams's comments. *Archbishop Martin.*

ARTS & PARTS

It's very hard to take something if you're not offered it. I have discovered there is a direct relationship between the people who say they wouldn't take it and those that are unlikely to be offered it. 'I wouldn't take that old stuff.' Well, you're not even in the running. *Theatre impresario Michael Colgan on the reaction to his accepting an honorary membership of the Order of the British Empire.*

Arts & parties

We've just survived the coldest winter in 30 years, the worst recession in 70 years appears to be, well, receding, and summer's just around the corner. Every year in the arts world seems a bit worse than the one that's just gone, but there are plenty of reasons to be cheerful, so we're going to party like it's 2007. *Seán Kelly, founding director of Belfast's Cathedral Quarter Arts Festival.*

Baton charge

You can't practise on your own. That would be ridiculous. Well, I suppose you could stand in front of the mirror and admire yourself in action. But that would be very, very silly. If you're going to conduct, you've got to conduct players. *David Brophy, principal conductor, RTÉ Concert Orchestra.*

Getting the picture

A film is a bit like writing a short story because you see it on one sitting, don't you? You can think it all through in your mind from start to finish, whereas a novel is something entirely different. *Writer and film-maker Neil Jordan.*

Professional fowl

It was a total accident. I was eating a chicken tikka sandwich and suddenly it worked for me. Having my mouth full of chicken tikka was the only way I could get Brian Cowen's voice. *Impersonator Mario Rosenstock.*

The importance of being Merlin

I tend to say Oscar was my grandfather, rather than saying I am his grandson. It's a subtle difference. *Oscar Wilde's lineal descendant Merlin Holland.*

HOME & AWAY

It's been very easy to settle here. The Aussies and the Irish are a very similar sort of people. Both nationalities are very laid back and don't really get too stressed about things. Every other Irish person at the moment keeps asking me, 'What are you doing here?' I suppose it seems like everyone is going the other way, but I definitely really enjoy living here. *Graphic designer David Scott.*

Beyond the beyonds

It's like having a small torch, putting it close to a stadium flood and see if you can see it a mile away. We're very lucky to be able to do this. People have been looking for planets around other planets for centuries and historically people have been burnt at the stake for this. To be in a position to do this, it is amazing what we can do. *Queen's University Professor Don Pollacco, Wide Angle Search for Planets.*

Put out more flags

If there is a hurling match going on, then every third car will have local colours. I think it points to a very different sense of national identity in Ireland. It's much more local here, and people are almost tribal in their perspective. Perhaps that's why the Tricolour doesn't get a look-in. *American author David Monagan.*

Up the pole

I have no problem with flying the Tricolour. But this one is sending out the wrong message. With the peace process, we are trying to promote friendship and good will. If someone put a Union Jack at Kilmainham Jail there would be a lot of people who wouldn't feel too happy about it. *Louth councillor Frank Godfrey on the flag placed on the Battle of the Boyne obelisk, an Orange shrine.*

An empire once again

We are certainly not going to shut the doors to the Irish, because the Irish, as far as we are concerned, are part of Britain and fully entitled to come here. *Nick Griffin, British National Party.*

People think there's no huge difference between Ireland and England but I can tell you it can be a different culture entirely at times. People don't realise how big an issue homesickness is, what a role it can play in whether a young lad makes it or not ... When you look at it, it's only a stretch of water but it can feel like a million miles. *Terry Conroy, FAI Player Welfare Officer in the UK.*

Underground movement

The reason we have bad congestion is that we don't have a metro. Traffic is a scourge but it isn't anything to do with car ownership; what really sets us apart from other cities of comparable size like Copenhagen, Stockholm or Munich is the public transport deficit. *Conor Faughnan, AA Roadwatch.*

LIP SERVICE

You kiss the babies, I'll kiss the mummies. *Sinn Féin's Gerry Kelly issues canvassing instructions to his party leader, Gerry Adams.*

You have breakfast with him, don't you?

'It doesn't get more intimate. You wake up in the morning and he's there, filling our head full of the silly and profound … He was a very serious intellect and a great analyst of the country's affairs, and then he had a potty mouth. He was a very irreverent man when dealing with serious topics.' Bono's tribute was one of a myriad paid to RTÉ's presenter Gerry Ryan from all sections of society on the occasion of his untimely death this month.

When someone comes to write the history of RTÉ and of broadcasting, they will have to devote a special analytical section to the phenomenon that was Gerry Ryan because he was in fact a phenomenon and an icon in the evolution of Irish broadcasting. *RTÉ chairman Tom Savage.*

As he lifted his glass, he brought the microphone close to his lips. Then he sipped the wine. He rolled it around his palate. He swallowed and sighed in satisfaction. His listeners could almost smell the bouquet. *David Blake Knox.*

In the early days of the programme we used to have to manufacture the stories. I remember a flying saucer near Bunclody, and also being the guy who had seen the ghost of a young girl on the Rock of Cashel. He used to get into trouble with management for that. He would be dragged in over it, and over the 'Three Old Men' because they didn't like the language or the innuendo, which wasn't very subtle! His attitude was 'Lads, we'll put it out and worry about it afterwards'—to me that was the great thing. He was more than a shock jock. He was a solicitor by trade and was very good at walking that line. He never landed them in court. *Writer John MacKenna, one of the 'Three Old Men' in an early RTÉ radio programme—the others were Joe Taylor and Gerry Ryan himself.*

PARTY LINES

I've only been elected for an hour and you want me to give it up? Give me a chance. *Gerry Adams, asked if this would be his last time standing in a British general election.*

Eons of Ians?

I never thought he'd lose. We Paisleys are made of stern stuff. But if he learned to be a politician from me, he learned to be a clever one from his mother. *Rev. Ian, as his son Ian Jnr is elected to succeed him in North Antrim.*

My father wants to live to 100. I don't know if people could stick him that long. *Ian Jnr.*

I think people would like to see an end to the Paisley dynasty, and not to have it pass on to another flawed generation. *Traditional Unionist Voice leader Jim Allister.*

Democratic deficit

I was just about to kiss my teddy bear goodnight and turn off the radio when Rachel English said word is coming in that Peter Robinson might be in trouble. *Journalist Brendan Keenan.*

Whatever is best for Northern Ireland, for the Democratic Unionist Party is my priority. If Peter Robinson walking into the sunset is best for Northern Ireland, for the Democratic Unionist Party, then that is what I would do. *The First Minister loses his Westminster seat.*

Perhaps both of us could leave the stage and allow a fresh leadership to look at the situation anew, without any baggage. If I can put myself in this position having failed to win a seat I'd never held, perhaps somebody who held their seat but lost it might think about his position. *Ulster Unionist leader Sir Reg Empey.*

The dog ate my homework

Late on the first day—you wouldn't get it in Low Babies. *Brian Hayes TD, on new Minister for Education Mary Coughlan missing her first session of ministerial questions.*

THE MEEJA

I remember years ago writing one of the first stories about Bertie and Celia. A week later I was at a book launch and I saw Bertie Ahern. He clocked me, and making a beeline for me, and I thought, 'Jesus, what's going to happen here?' Bertie said, 'Hiya Paddy. I remember you used to write industrial relations stories for the paper. I've just been made responsible for labour, so if you want to talk about anything, just give me a call. Here's my number.' He didn't even mention my story. My jaw was just hanging off me. It was the first time I realised what a calculating professional he was. *Phoenix editor Paddy Prendiville.*

To Di for

It did sort of veer towards the Princess Di idea, which I did find bizarre. There seems to be a default position for media that if you have a celebrity death, we cover it like we covered Princess Di, but he was a different sort of person to Princess Di. To treat him as a Di figure was bizarre. *Michael Foley, Department of Journalism, DIT, on the media coverage of the death of Gerry Ryan.*

Holy no-show

The modern communications media provide great opportunities but there is no way that the renewal of the church will be achieved just by slick media gestures and soundbites. The message of Jesus is too deep to be encapsulated into soundbites. Indeed, a priority of the process of proclaiming the Gospel is that of taking people beyond the soundbite culture. *Archbishop of Dublin Diarmuid Martin.*

Sky in the pie

We are discussing something very important here—the access and full participation of Irish people, regardless of income or location, to important sporting events. This is about sports for all. *Minister Eamon Ryan advocates free-to-air television for important rugby and other matches.*

Does he want that on his head that he personally brought down Irish rugby on the back of a hunch? It is up to us as a governing body to decide that. It's not up to the Minister. *IRFU chief executive Philip Browne.*

I think there's a strong argument to have free-to-air. The State has put a huge amount of money into the IRFU and soccer to provide them with a stadium. Rugby is very big in Limerick where I come from. If you went to the pub to see the Munster-Leinster game last Saturday, the pub was full of families with young kids. There's something very wrong about that. *Niall Collins, TD and former Garryowen player.*

No comment
I'm sick of journalists endlessly spouting their opinions. Fundamentally, we're reflectors, we're not at the core of events. *Incoming RTÉ Washington correspondent Richard Downes.*

BRICKS & MORTAR

I'm a big fan of the new stadium. It dominates the view from the back window of our kitchen and bedroom. Initially we were concerned about how it might affect our light, but as it's mostly a transparent structure it's even a bit of an improvement on that front, compared to the old stadium. I like the design, and I love the way it kinks down at our end. It reminds me of a bedpan! *Journalist and author Gerard Siggins on developments at Lansdowne Road, Dublin.*

I've always said the proudest moment of my life was leading the Irish team out on to the old Lansdowne Road. In saying that, it was always a bit treacherous coming up the old steps and you felt a bit like Bambi on stilts. *Former Irish rugby captain Keith Wood.*

Two cheers for the Palindrome
Now that the new stadium is finished I don't object to the design but I think it is just far too big for the site; it should have been built out at Abbotstown. It dominates the landscape here and it dominated my line of vision. One of the main arguments for redeveloping the stadium here was because of the history associated with Lansdowne Road and the name. But now it's called Aviva—so it could be anywhere. *Local resident Séamus Kelly.*

Fair city

The washing machine empties onto the floor. You can't go out when it's on because you'd be afraid what you'd come back to. And the smell ... you wouldn't get it in a slum. *Sinéad Martin, Dolphin House flats, Dublin.*

I was told I wasn't to use 'fancy' toilet paper. Dublin City Council told me that if I used three-ply I would block the toilet and they wouldn't come out to me to fix it. *Veronica Lally, Dolphin House.*

Lift off

For the past twelve months we have only had lifts for five weeks that are working. I live on the fifth floor, and I suffer from fibromyalgia, arthritis and diabetes, as well as having a slipped disc. So when I go to get my groceries every morning, I am relying on someone's generosity to help me down and to get back up to the fifth floor. It is crazy. *Catherine Mulvihill, Ballymun flats, Dublin.*

ARTS & PARTS

Call me old-fashioned but I believe that my job is to reveal a rich text for what it is: a deeply human thing. It is about emotional engagement as well as intellectual stimulation. It is about animating the depth of character and action in these false worlds. It is life lived more intensely for two hours. *Theatre producer Patrick Mason.*

Part of what we aren't

Three consecutive Eurovision victories were a source of national pride and self-confidence for Ireland, and may even have helped getting investment capital from countries abroad. They have certainly engendered a considerable growth in tourism figures. Eurovision helped to transmit a cliché of Irishness that is still considered very positive in the rest of Europe. *Academic Eurovision observer Irving Wolther.*

Domestic drama

Both my parents were extremely passionate about plays. The real drama was that they had different tastes, and their rows were like something from the theatre, him shouting O'Casey at her, her giving him Shakespeare back. It was like some great play. *Playwright Bernard Farrell.*

SOCIAL & PERSONAL

We're calling for the State to recognise the non-Catholic people who were buried and born in the same circumstances as a lot of the Catholic people that were compensated under the redress scheme. We want our home to be added on to the list of institutions in order to qualify for the scheme so that children who were buried here in 1935 can get the recognition. *Derek Leinster, Bethany House Survivors' Group, Dublin.*

Embattlement
Here we have a guy with a castle, with horses, with private fishing rights and a beneficiary of tax breaks calling for the lowest-paid workers in the country to be paid even less. Not only is this guy blue-blooded but he sounds pretty cold-blooded as well, and the Blarney he speaks doesn't impress me one iota. *Cork councillor Mick Barry on Blarney Castle owner Charles Colthurst.*

When we sported and played
The freedom of childhood has been lost. While many great strides have been made in areas such as health and nutrition especially, the freedom of childhood is gone. We all have memories of meandering and playing and not coming home until the tea was ready, but now those days are over. *Irene Gunning, Irish Pre-school Play Association.*

HIS & HERS

You do get a few negative comments, but nothing serious. People might shout across the road, 'Hey, pull up your pants.' I think the idea of banning them is crazy—it's like trying to ban certain hairstyles. *Cork barman Kane Murphy defends a prevailing fashion for droopy drawers.*

Bagging Mr Big
Irish women became very snobby in the type of man they were looking for. Lots of women were disappointed that they could go into Brown Thomas and buy a designer handbag for €5,000 but they couldn't find a man who was just as fabulous ... In the current environment, a civil servant or tradesman with a steady, pensionable job will suddenly seem a lot more attractive to women than a potless property developer. *Relationship expert David Kavanagh.*

Cupid's DART

I think we are gentle greenies and when we decided we were going to get married in the registry office, the easiest and the most sensible thing to do was to get the train. *Josephine McDonnell, on the journey from Dún Laoghaire to Grand Canal Dock, Dublin, to wed Australian Jim Sheer.*

Crisp rejoinder

Everything is so serious and gloomy now and we want to inject a little bit of fun into things. *Largo Foods' Raymond Coyle on his Hunky Dory poster campaign featuring generous examples of female pulchritude.*

It's really tiresome to see companies resorting to this kind of old-style sexism when the world is full of so many imaginative possibilities. *Susan McKay, National Women's Council.*

Silenced sisters

We've hardly said one full sentence and we're interrupted, whereas the men seem to get away with going on a lot longer before they are told they shouldn't be talking. *Jan Sullivan TD detects a sexist attitude on the part of the Ceann Comhairle.*

Beyond the pail

On the water question, you can thank the Irish Countrywomen's Association because they carried out a campaign for water in the home and urged rural women not to marry a farmer unless he installed water in his house as well as his byre. He thought it a fine idea to put it into his byre, but 'why would you be bothered putting it into the kitchen, wasn't she well fit to carry a few buckets' sort of attitude. *Women's activist Mamo McDonald.*

Joint venture

I suppose it wasn't completely out of the blue. I kind of expected it. We were supposed to go to New York for my 30th birthday in January but we couldn't find the time until the May bank holiday. It was lovely. Paul proposed in Central Park—he didn't go down on one knee because he's not your traditional type. Anyway, he has bad knees. *Lucinda Creighton TD on her betrothal to Senator Paul Bradford.*

Add lib

Eavan Boland, my good friend the poet, was a member of the Women's Liberation Movement, and she rang me up one day and said, 'Mary, could you give me seven laws that discriminate against women.' And I said, 'Why seven, Eavan, I can give you nine or even ten?' She said, 'No, no, no, seven's a good number, and I want to go in today and we will try and fight these seven points.' I didn't have difficulty identifying seven laws ... *Former lawyer and President of Ireland Mary Robinson.*

Fatted calf

I'm going to talk to you today about Irish women's fear of their legs. *Fashion journalist Constance Harris on RTÉ's 'Arena'.*

FADÓ, FADÓ

People like Tom Barrington were writing in the 1950s about how this is a very badly governed country. There's a dearth of ideas and a devotion to old ways of doing things. And that's rooted in the early years of the State. A revolution is an opportunity to think about new ways of doing things but it quickly became clear in our case that that wasn't going to happen. *Historian Diarmaid Ferriter.*

Gael force

These Irish speakers were the backbone of the post-Famine Belfast Gaeltacht at the centre of a busy Victorian Irish city. At its height there were up to 300 people living in the Gaeltacht quarter and living their lives through Irish. They would travel throughout the city on a daily basis on painted carts selling their own produce, much of which had come from their native Omeath. Many of their descendants went on to open up fishmongers as well as fruit and veg shops in the years that followed. Some of the city's best-known traders today can trace their ancestors right back to those first Irish speakers from Omeath. *Professor Fionntán de Brún.*

FUN & GAMES

If someone turned around to me now and said, 'You're going to finish your career with ten Majors,' obviously I'd be ecstatic. Would I be disappointed if Rory won eleven? And would I be happier if I won nine Majors in total and Rory won eight? Then I'd be happier if I won ten Majors and Rory won eleven, rather than me winning nine and Rory winning eight. *Golfer Pádraig Harrington explains.*

After the ball

Often a player would take the money from his testimonial and buy a pub. All of the players from before 1986 had to find jobs. Some have gone on to manage clubs, but just being a footballer doesn't qualify you to manage a club, so what are you qualified to do? The answer, quite honestly, is nothing. *Belfast photographer Michael Donald, who has taken pictures of every living World Cup final scorer.*

Survival was always the name of the game for me, when you've been poor, when you've been a footballer, when you've had to finish your career at 33 and do something else, the objective was always survival. I'd still be in that mode. Survival on my own terms, though, without having to kiss anybody's ass, Tony O'Reilly's or Denis O'Brien's or anybody else. *Broadcaster and soccer commentator Eamon Dunphy.*

All hands on deck

Poker's all about people. You get dealt a hand and the first mistake you can make is to think that this is all about the hand that *you* have, but the hand that *you* have is only a very small part of the equation—everybody else is getting dealt a hand as well. *Professional poker player Padraig Parkinson.*

London pride

Work at home was getting quiet and I was playing football, but I wasn't getting anywhere. This evening it took me two-and-a-half hours to drive 40 miles. Everyone is pretty much in the same boat. It seems to mean an awful lot more to people playing over here than it does in Ireland. Everybody makes a big effort to play, so there is a lot more enjoyment in it. You get a lot of friends out of it and it's a close-knit group. *Former Galway player Paul Geraghty on the London GAA scene.*

Because it's there

The challenge I went through, I'm convinced people are going to be killed at that. If you talk to any merchant seaman who has been out on tankers, they thought I was mad. And people will tell you that you are mad, but you still do it. But I'm convinced that people will be killed at that challenge. It's horrific out there. I would tell them, don't do it, that it's madness and too dangerous, but the type of person that's going to do it, it doesn't matter what I say, they are still going to do it. *Rower Seán McGowan, first Irishman to cross the Atlantic solo.*

Palpable hit

I'm the kind of person that if I see a ball coming in my direction I don't stand there ... I'll pick up whatever instrument is to hand, be it a hockey stick, a hurley stick or a cricket bat and I'll give it a wind, see if I can score. You have to take your opportunities. *Putative presidential candidate David Norris.*

'ATIN' & DRINKIN'

If the government continues to enact legislation that forces people out of the controlled environment of the pub and into the unregulated environment of the home to drink, that will eventually lead to serious alcohol abuse. *Gerry Mellet, Vintners' Federation of Ireland.*

Baaa, humbug!

It's impossible to get mutton, it's a struggle. You've to fight with a butcher nowadays to get mutton to make an Irish stew. They will concede that it's year-old lamb and you can call it mutton. That's only a marketing thing. I know mutton by the smell of it. I don't have to be told either. There is a distinctive taste and smell of mutton. It's different to lamb. *Senator Joe O'Toole.*

Could you tell mutton dressed as lamb? *Senator John Paul Phelan.*

I know mutton dressed up as lamb and lamb dressed up as mutton. I am lucky to be of a generation that has learned that great art and I worry about young men who never get to make the distinction. *Senator O'Toole.*

Uno agus uno

I think what the Irish people like—the potato. Things are probably changing now that they've sampled pasta, but spuds were the staple diet. The culture is changing and the youth of today travel a lot more. I remember being in school, and the furthest the lads would go is west of the Shannon, but now there isn't a teenager who hasn't been out of the country. But for me, spuds will always be the national dish of Ireland, be they mashed, boiled or in chips. *Mario Aprile, Irish Traditional Italian Chipper Association.*

HOME & AWAY

The whole cast look forward to the Irish shows throughout the entire tour—it is like the sweetest wine and the greatest homecoming. They have families in the audience. When I am behind the curtain on opening night in Dublin, I will be on my knee waiting for the curtain to open and I will be able to summon up all those great memories. *'Riverdance' creator Michael Flatley.*

I said to my mother-in-law recently that Dublin used to bounce and sparkle, and now it just feels like a kind of worn energy that I haven't ever experienced before. *Former 'Riverdance' dancer Jean Butler.*

Off centre
When the decentralisation was proposed we warned that it would create inefficiency, and that has turned out to be true. Many civil servants spend long hours travelling between meetings. There are civil servants who have to attend meetings in Brussels. Because they are now based down the country, it takes them many more hours to get there. *Dave Thomas, Association of Higher Civil and Public Servants.*

Ar mhuin na muice
Back in my grandad's time, the hotel was almost incidental to the farm. There was a pig farm, so any left-over food was given to the pigs. Then we were just open four months a year. Tourism was very different. Irish people didn't really go on holidays—you'd go and see your auntie and uncle or something like that, in Cork or Kerry, and that was your holiday. This idea of going away on your holidays was something new. *Bill Kelly, Kelly's Hotel, Rosslare.*

CRIME & PUNISHMENT

Mountjoy is 160 years old; it's falling down. On Tuesday we had 670 inmates. The inspector of prisons said it should be 540. It's a long way off that. You cannot do anything with people in that situation except warehousing; end of story. *Governor John Lonergan.*

It is not acceptable that people are confined to cells because of overcrowding. The whole point is to rehabilitate people in prison and this cannot happen when they can't access training or other facilities. There is also a human rights issue. These people have not been convicted to be sent to a virtual solitary confinement and they are entitled to exercise and some freedom of movement. *Aengus Ó Snodaigh TD.*

The majority of women have children to quite a few partners—so they do a lot of worrying inside. Women are more vocal. You'll hear hospital nurses say it's more difficult to work in a women's ward, because women worry. It could be about the home, bills, is the corporation going to take the house and are the kids going to be taken into care? And then, of course, there's the whole worry about communions, confirmations, Christmas—about paying for them. Those are the times when they would go into prostitution. *Katherine McMahon, retiring governor, Dóchas women's prison, Dublin.*

Head count
As gardaí, we saw head shops as the most significant element of policing from a negative perspective that we had seen in many years and one which had the potential to create more damage than anything seen from a drugs perspective previously. It had the potential to do that in such double-quick time that we had never seen it before. *Chief Superintendent Pat Leahy in the wake of the government ban on specified drugs.*

AG OBAIR

Staying focused is never an issue and remaining attentive is not a problem, because whatever else they might be, surgical procedures are never boring. Most surgeons are driven by their own internal make-up, and in general we are at our best when operating. But surgeons also vary in their ability to remain calm—some prefer drama and tension, but most like calmness throughout, and learning how to achieve this is something that gets refined over the years. *Corkman Edward Kiely, leader of the London team that separated the Cork conjoined twins.*

Oh, les beaux jours

When I was Ireland's worst library assistant, banished to the mobile libraries, we would stop in Donabate for an old lady called Isabella Lucinda Bright who always loved two detective novels and something by Beckett— because he made her laugh. He does the same to me. *Writer Dermot Bolger.*

Hammerklavier

Since the Celtic Tiger—God rest its soul—it is really hard to fine good places to record duos and small ensembles. For bigger gigs we have a box at the National Concert Hall, but we can really only use it for the orchestras because it is too expensive for us to hire independently. Small venues that used to be good now tend to have motorways built next to them. For one project, we had picked out four possible churches in Cork, but three of them were in the middle of building sites. Jackhammers, trucks going past, the whole works. *Lyric FM CD producer Eoin Brady.*

Offaly pleased

There was a huge buzz around the town when it was announced. People were delighted. This was going to be the salvation of Birr. I always knew it was pie in the sky that 400 staff would come down from Dublin. Everyone in Birr would have liked to see that, but now we know that it is a dead duck. *Councillor Michael Campbell on the promise of the decentralisation of the training agency FÁS.*

Sweet nothings

Daily, I wander through my city with a trolley and a cardboard box full of dreams and I hear the crashing of other people's jobs all around me. My most treasured possession is that I've got nothing to lose. *Dublin street poet Pat Ingoldsby.*

MAMMON

It's an infectious feeling when you are down there presenting the cheque. The one thing you notice when people win is the relief that comes with financial security. It is the relief that the worry of paying mortgages and losing their job is over. In many ways, the recession is over for them once they win the jackpot. *Dermot Griffin, chief executive, National Lottery.*

Told you so

In spring 2006 we argued that fiscal policy was too lax. That summer we raised questions about the sustainability of the economy in regard to the size of the construction sector. In winter 2006 we pointed out that the budget was too expansionary. In spring 2007 we discussed serious concerns on the growth trajectory. The theme of autumn 2007 was uncertainty. We mentioned the potential for a banking collapse. In winter 2007 we discussed the unsustainable nature of a recent growth experience. In the spring of 2008 we warned about deterioration in public finances, and the need to curtail spending. Then, that summer, the R word. *John FitzGerald, ESRI, challenging the claim of David McWilliams that he was the first economist to cry wolf.*

Hard drive

When we get a company executive over from California, we put him in a car to Westport, and by the time he gets to Ballaghaderreen he's looking out the window thinking he's in a Third World country. It's embarrassing and it makes it almost impossible to argue for any further investment here. *Pat O'Donnell, Mayo Industries Group.*

Pilot error

I am unable to read properly. I believe that I suffer from dyslexia, although I have had reading difficulties from an early age and left school early due to this. *Millionaire businessman Jim Mansfield Jnr claims in court that he did not understand the obligations in a €6.2 million loan agreement.*

It's extraordinary that a person who can't read is able to fly a helicopter. *Mr Justice Peter Kelly.*

CREATURES GREAT & SMALL

If we cannot discuss scientific articles about topics directly related to our own research, published in leading peer-reviewed international journals with colleagues in the same department, this bodes very ill for informed inquiry and debate. *UCC lecturer Dr Dylan Evans, the subject of a complaint of sexual harassment by a female colleague over his showing her a research paper that finds that fruit bats perform oral sex on each other.*

Obviously it's about context here, and if I had gone around in some sort of leering manner saying to people, 'Oh, look at this, fruit bats are doing something dodgy here, ha ha, nudge, nudge, wink, wink,' then yes, clearly that would be reprehensible. *Dr Evans arís.*

Ark de triomphe

Protecting our biodiversity is a complex matter but nonetheless some of our projects have had great success: the Golden Eagle Project: in spite of difficulties with poisoning, we have re-introduced Red Kites to Wicklow, Golden Eagles to Donegal and White-Tailed Eagles to Kerry; we have provided new breeding ponds for the Natterjack Toad in Kerry; the numbers for the Peregrine Falcon are noted at an historic high; the Grey Partridge, which was near extinction, now has a viable population; bats are generally in good status and we have relocated red squirrels to the west in order to afford them protection from the grey squirrel. *Green Party minister John Gormley.*

There's lots of farmers living with them for three years now. I've seen kite nests very close to habitats. There was one ten miles from a farmer's house. One farmer said during the snows he was feeding them venison and sheep carcases. *Damien Clarke, Red Kite Project.*

Phoenix pork?

When is the last time you saw a pig in a field? In 1840, there were 350,000 pigs in Ireland kept on under an acre. I was looking at an old Ordnance Survey map of Dublin and kept seeing 'piggery' on the map. There is massive potential for reintroducing pigs to Dublin, particularly in those old council houses that have huge gardens. I wanted to experience meat production and be an honest carnivore. *Ella McSweeney, Blackrock, Co. Dublin, RTÉ presenter and pig-keeper*

Furry tales

Sharon Ní Bheoláin is the Labrador person. Anne Doyle is cats. I'll take anything. Four legs and a tail and you are sure of a good meal and somewhere to put your head. As a child, if anyone was looking for me, my late mother would tell them, 'Look no further than the nearest dog and you'll find her.' *Actress and animal lover Linda Martin.*

NOT HIS PROVINCE

In the end you can always do a deal with an Ulsterman, but it's not the way to run a modern sophisticated society. *British Conservative MP Ken Clarke.*

What happened should never, ever have happened

—*said British Prime Minister David Cameron: 'Some members of our armed forces acted wrongly. The government is ultimately responsible for the conduct of the armed forces, and for that, on behalf of the government, indeed on behalf of our country, I am deeply sorry.' The publication of the Saville Report on the events of Bloody Sunday thirty-eight years ago, and this belated apology, are welcomed by nearly all shades of opinion in Ireland and beyond.*

Today is the day when the truth has been set free in the city of Derry. This is not about the reopening of old wounds but rather it is about the healing of the gaping wounds of injustice left behind by the terrible events of Bloody Sunday. The brave and honest words of Prime Minister David Cameron in the House of Commons today will echo round the world. *Taoiseach Brian Cowen.*

This massive expenditure on politically motivated inquiries whilst thousands of other victims see nothing spent on obtaining any degree of truth or justice surrounding the deaths of their loved ones is not acceptable, nor is it sympathetic to the loved ones who still seek justice. *DUP MP Gregory Campbell.*

We see it as anyone attacking the inquiry as attacking the families. This is a human rights issue. It is not about the republican or political aspect; it's about what happened on the day. My younger brother died on a civil rights march that day; he did not die fighting for a united Ireland. He was walking on a peaceful civil rights march when his life was taken from him by a paratrooper. *John Kelly.*

It's brilliant. It's fantastic for Derry and I think it has united everybody … It's united a lot of people on both sides because the nationalist community knew what had happened, but on the other side of the divide a lot of people thought what happened was the fault of the people, and it's great just to get that cleared up. *Clare Miller, Derry.*

We, as loyalists, must appreciate the tenacity of the Bogsiders in pursuing their aims and learn from them that 38 years is never too long to pursue an inquiry. *Orange Order member Tom Haire.*

CÓRAS IOMPAIR

I know of elderly people who had been living just three or four miles outside a village who sold their homes to move in closer when they were forced to give up driving. They felt that without their cars they were scuppered and that they'd no other options … For every one of them, it means they are no longer an autonomous human being. From that moment they're dependent on family, neighbours, friends and public transport. Families need to be as sensitive as possible to the changing needs of parents who can no longer drive. They need to remember that it's not enough to take the car keys away and then go home. *Gerry Scully, Age Action Ireland.*

Excira' and delira'

I'm absolutely thrilled. It's a big occasion opening a motorway of any sort. It's particularly a proud moment for me—I'm here in my own county. It's just fantastic. *Minister for Transport Noel Dempsey at the opening of the M3 motorway.*

Road rage

The desecration of the landscape around Tara was shameful, short-sighted and beyond belief. *Writer Colm Tóibín disapproves.*

SICKNESS & HEALTH

I can still remember, five years on, that sense of total inner panic and fear that came right through me when my doctor said to me that one of the six sample tests which took place in Tallaght was cancerous. *Ruairí Quinn TD.*

You can see tribunals about this in 20 years' time. The degree to which pride is invested in winning school cups in all the provinces is excessive. *Professor Brendan Buckley, Irish anti-doping committee, on coaches who encourage young sportsmen to use supplements.*

She's at the most advanced stage now ... She can't communicate. She uses words but not in any real sequence. We've gone through our trauma, we still have Florence with us, but she's in a nursing home now. We're not doing the caring, we're visiting—and we think about it, and we talk about it. We've gone through it, but there are some families that are at the end of their tether—and they need help. *Michael Noonan TD on his wife's struggle with Alzheimer's disease.*

HIS & HERS

It has been a very long road and at times I thought it would never end, but I felt I just had to keep going for my own dignity and self-respect and for all the other transgender people out there who were suffering in silence. *Dr Lydia Foy wins the right to be officially recognised as a woman.*

Male disorder

What I hate about the World Cup is that no woman is going to have any attention from any males in this country for the next few weeks. Texts will be ignored. Dates will be cancelled. Plans will be changed. I will get aggravated by all the hype. Every conversation is going to be taken up with football. *Róisín Conlan, Marino, Dublin.*

Cooking up a storm

Working with your partner is not easy, and anyone who says otherwise is lying. You know the way they say you have to keep things fresh? Well, it's never fresh. In a kitchen, the pressures of time, heat and customer demands are all against you. You've got to look at your work relationship coldly and try not to get emotionally involved. I treat Sallyanne like any other colleague. Sometimes I have to bite my tongue not to say something to her because I don't want to pay for it later—other chefs who work with their missus will know what I mean! *Dublin chef Derry Clarke.*

PARTY LINES

I could take you to the Ballymena Town Council and show you how they do it. That there was a genteel performance. *On a visit to Dublin, Rev. Ian Paisley is not too impressed by rowdy scenes in the Dáil.*

Ivor/or

It is such a cute hoor stroke, like something Pat Shortt would have dreamed up. I felt he was arrogantly thumbing his nose at the rest of us, as if nobody knows whether he lived in Clontarf or West Cork. *John Mulligan, Boyle, Co. Roscommon, on the controversy over the two residences claimed on expenses by Senator Ivor Callely.*

I had to get out of Clontarf. Fairly soon after the election I went to Cork, to our holiday home, and I stayed there. I was there when Bertie appointed me to the Senate. As far as I was concerned, that was where I was living. I didn't want to come back to Clontarf. I stayed there in Cork for a considerable period of time. I may have been up and down for the Senate. I may have spent a night in Clontarf, or somewhere else in Dublin. But as far as I was concerned, I was based in Cork. *Ivor Callely elucidates.*

He's been coming here since he was a young fellow—wasn't his mother from here?—that's the connection. Quote me? Are you serious? Don't ye twist everything. Ye media are all the same. *Determinedly anonymous Kilcrohane, Co. Cork, resident.*

Fianna Fáil takes this issue very seriously and believes that it must be addressed comprehensively and transparently. *Taoiseach Brian Cowen.*

Push comes to shove

People have been looking to see Enda present a convincing case that he can manage the economic problems and he can secure people's future and he has the capacity to reform and implement that reform. I think he has been found wanting on that. *Richard Bruton challenges Enda Kenny's leadership of Fine Gael.*

I spoke to Richard again today. And during these conversations I tried to persuade him that he should desist from any action that would inflict damage on the Fine Gael party and as a consequence on our supporters. He confirmed to me that he could no longer support me, and in that context I am placed in an impossible position of moving a motion of no confidence in the Taoiseach in the Dáil tomorrow and cannot have a situation where my deputy leader does not offer his support for me. *Enda Kenny*

Molly Bloom's soliloquy is a wonderfully apposite thing this year. I believe Richard Bruton has passed out the soliloquy to all his followers, and they are all saying, 'Yes I will yes!' *Writer and historian Tim Pat Coogan.*

SOCIAL & PERSONAL

Going to Summerhill was a total culture shock. People lived in tenement flats. There'd be eight families living in one house. That place was crawling with rats—rats the size of kittens, immune to every poison ever invented. Parents would talk about waking in the morning and finding a rat on the baby's cot. There was no sound-proofing and you'd hear every word from the other rooms. Summerhill was used by Dublin Corporation as a sort of dumping ground for families who'd been evicted from other areas. *Fr Peter McVerry, founder of a hostel for homeless boys.*

Day job
In Dublin now, over 45 per cent of all funerals do not have an evening removal. There is no religious basis for it. It was brought in in the early twentieth century so people didn't have to take time off work to attend. It's a typically Irish thing. I think people don't want to have to go through the performance twice. Once is enough—shaking hands and saying hello to people. *Gus Nichols, Irish Association of Funeral Directors.*

Quid pro quo
The secret is this: I was nice to everyone and everyone was nice to me. *106-year-old Paddy Gleeson, O'Callaghan's Mills, Co. Clare, asked the secret of a long life.*

ARTS & PARTS

Eamon made a career as a kind of thuggish iconoclast. It is not a style I like, and he has made so many U-turns, I don't know if I accept the integrity of a lot of the positions he has taken. Eamon did a vitriolic column in the *Sunday Independent* and then did fawning interviews on radio with people he had excoriated in the press. That was, I suspect, a pragmatic choice … *Derek Davis on Eamon Dunphy.*

Dr who?
If you had asked me at any time in the last 70 or 80 years, or whatever I am, who would be the least likely candidate for a doctorate in UCC, I would have said 'me.' And if I had actually gone to college, I would have said 'I.' *Actor Niall Tóibín at his conferral.*

On song
I can't sing a note but I know what's nice. We look for someone who sounds as close as possible to the original artist but who can also put on a show. You can be the best singer in the world but a terrible performer. It's about the full package … The opinion poll augurs very well for a Labour-led government. I will be looking for Arts and Culture on account of my experience. *Kathleen Lynch TD, chosen as a judge at the world karaoke championships in Moscow.*

Funny business
Doing a festival, it reminds you of just how much overlap there is in subject matter. It always reminds me of that village called Muff and they have a diving school there. Every comic who finds that out thinks they're the first one with it … *Comedian Kevin Bridges.*

One of the things which appears to be in vogue right now is to quote comedians' lines which are said in context with a certain amount of delivery and irony in a live room and just dictate it onto the page and write that up as controversial or shocking. I think the easiest thing, or maybe even the laziest thing, in the world is to get a controversial headline just by purely quoting what people on stage say rather than how they say it or what wry look there may have been when they were saying it. *Comedian Patrick Kielty.*

When people ask you what you do, and you say you're a comic, and they say, 'Tell us a joke, then,' I ask them what they do. If the person says, 'I'm a bricklayer', I say, 'Build us a wall then.' *Comedian Willie White.*

I had a couple of prison warden jokes that went down a storm. But I went directly back into my usual material then and I lost the connection. There's a rule in comedy that when a performance goes badly, it's never the audience's fault. And nowhere was this ever truer. These guys wanted to laugh more than anything in the world. But I didn't fulfil my end of the bargain. *Comedian Jarlath Regan on performing a prison gig.*

Leaking lady

Underneath the sequins in the *gúna*, you kind of adopt a sumo-wrestler posture when you sing a high note. You spread your legs and drop your pelvis. It is one of those arias where you can really pee in your pants. We do. It's a huge issue with singers. It's very physical, so make sure you get a toilet break before you sing high, otherwise you're in trouble. *Soprano Cara O'Sullivan.*

I contact

In a concert you sing out to the audience, you invite them in by your charisma and your stage presence; you can look around, you can feel everybody. With the opera, you have to engage people in a different way. You have to kind of bring them in, as opposed to going out to get them. You have to draw them in. Sometimes you can feel it. *Soprano Celine Byrne.*

Polytechnique

It's an uplifting experience. I tell my students not to worry if they make a mistake, they can always cut a section off, glue on another bit of polystyrene, cover it and no one would ever notice the difference. *Gerard Bedell, sculptor in polystyrene at Belfast Crescent Arts Centre.*

Given the bird

I told him how much I enjoyed it and he almost ate the face off me. He said it was ridiculous of me to be praising such a silly book. *Actor Eamon Morrissey recalls attempting to congratulate Flann O'Brien on his novel* At Swim-Two-Birds.

HERE & THERE

The lesson I've learnt about travel is that it's not enough. It's not enough to pass through, you have to pass in. In 2003, I went to stay with an Inuit shaman, way up in polar Alaska, where the Bering and the Chukchi seas meet. To me it was 'The Big Lonely'. It took me and a guide three days to find him, and I stayed for a month, sleeping in the same room. Like my incarceration in Lebanon, time meant nothing in that light-filled wilderness. *Former hostage Brian Keenan.*

Home brew
In Peter Barry I believe we have a man that embodies all that is best about Cork people. Peter Barry sums up the very many great elements we have in our society and in our people. We put great stock in Cork in family business. There probably is no family business that sums up Cork better than Barry's Tea. *Cork Lord Mayor Dara Murphy, presenting the former Tánaiste with the freedom of the city.*

We are a proud people. We are not the capital city and I don't think we should aspire to be the capital city. We are unique in ourselves. *Peter Barry, responding.*

Ship to shore
We have called for the unconditional release of Irish citizens currently detained in Ashdod. These did not enter Israel illegally, they were plucked out of international waters and brought to Ashdod. They don't need to sign any documents as far as we are concerned. *Foreign Minister Mícheál Martin on the seizure of crew members aboard the* Rachel Corrie *carrying a humanitarian cargo to Gaza.*

They took our clothes away, so showering without clean clothes wasn't much fun. I expected to be scared. I worried about my courage, but when you are faced with it, the anger and outrage makes you courageous. The arrogance of these characters threatening Irish citizens on the high seas; it was a hijack and a kidnap, it was bizarre. *Former UN Assistant Secretary-General Denis Halliday.*

We would go back, of course—the international community, we all have a role to play to tell this story. *Crew member and Nobel laureate Mairéad Corrigan Maguire.*

Pole position

Bronislaw Komorowski visited London but he treated both islands as a whole. And the immigration patterns in Ireland are different—a lot of Polish come here for a couple of years and go back, whilst our fellow countrymen in Britain tend to stay there for life. I would suggest the candidates to remember the Polish in Ireland. *Polish ambassador to Ireland Tadeusz Szumowski on canvassing for the forthcoming election.*

CHURCH & STATE

The failure to agree a community relations agenda and community relations strategy is, in my view, a public disgrace, given our history. That disgrace is heightened by the apparent failure of much wider society to even be concerned about it, never mind outraged by it. There is a problem with sectarianism right across much of Northern Ireland and it is acute in what might be seen as some very surprising places. *Presbyterian Moderator Dr Norman Hamilton.*

Windsor not

Sinn Féin opposes the proposed visit of the Queen of England, commander-in-chief of the British armed forces. Until there is complete withdrawal of the British military and the British administration from Ireland, and until there is justice and truth for victims of collusion, no official welcome should be accorded to any officer of the British armed forces of any rank. *Caoimhghín Ó Caoláin TD.*

I think that would be a good development. I think also that the importance of an exchange of state visits says a lot about the modern bilateral relationships we now have. *Taoiseach Brian Cowen.*

We have written to the Palace offering to carry her for free, which is the way most people now travel to Ireland. We hope that she will accept our very kind offer. In her case we will make an exception—we'll waive the excess baggage fee. We'll even waive the one carry-on bag rule. *Ryanair's Michael O'Leary.*

Exit poll

We thought that maybe 100 people would want to do it, but it turned out there was a huge response ... I still can't get over it. I was probably naïve. We're clearing out the dead wood, in a sense. We're not culling the herd, we're not getting rid of staunch believers. We're getting rid of people who aren't fully on board. *Gráinne O'Sullivan, co-founder of the web site 'Count Me Out', assisting the disaffected to leave the Catholic Church.*

'ATIN' & DRINKIN'

I remember it so well. I thought we'd had a really bad week in the three places. Turnover had dropped by 25, 30 per cent. Nobody was having the extras. There was no glass of champagne before the meal. There were no Armagnacs after the meal. People were coming in and having three glasses of wine instead of ordering the bottle. *Black July 2008, as recalled by formerly successful Dublin restaurateur Ronan Ryan.*

Orange order

Raspberry jam and marmalade are the things I do most. The marmalade has to be made from proper Seville oranges, mind, none of your canned stuff ... I buy the oranges fresh and freeze them for when I need to make a new batch. *Richard Bruton TD reveals an unexpected talent.*

Bleu blood

Just inside the door there was a table on the right known as the Royal Box. I was working one lunchtime when word spread around the kitchen ... Peter Ustinov is in the Royal Box! I didn't actually serve him but one day I was told to take a double fillet steak cooked *bleu*, that is hardly cooked at all, to a table and I discovered I was serving Orson Welles. *Patrick Anthony, former boy waiter at the legendary Restaurant Jammet, Dublin.*

MEEJA

The only thing I don't like about this programme is oftentimes there's a reaction from the disciplinary bodies to things that we might say on the television about different players. They should make up their own minds on things. It shouldn't have to be pointed out to them on 'The Sunday Game' whether or not a player was guilty of foul play or not. *Panellist Colm O'Rourke.*

Taking a rise

It's funny, Radio 1 can have that effect on people. It's amazing. You take something that is really well established, and you move it to another time, and the whole country kind of goes out of sync. It's like, say, when Marian Finucane moved from weekdays to weekends. People would hear her on a Saturday morning and jump out of bed, thinking they were late, but after a while we settle back down again. *Presenter John Creedon.*

Madam and evil

Much as I am an admirer of the *Irish Times* and indeed I wrote a column for it for four years, it's also quite a dangerous paper. It bounced Garret FitzGerald into a divorce referendum in 1986 by, in my opinion, a wholly misleading opinion poll. *Minister of State Martin Mansergh.*

Papers like the *Irish Times*, and the authenticity they supply, are worth a lot to the public. The more scabrous sites don't carry anything like the conviction that a paper provides. I read the *Irish Times* this morning and I took it almost as gospel. I believed it. That is the foundation of great newspapers. *Veteran newspaper editor Harold Evans.*

MAMMON

There is no such thing as a tax exile. There are a huge number of Irish people who work abroad and retain an Irish residence. If you take people who work for multinationals and so on, technically speaking they are outside Ireland for the required number of days … There are nurses who do that. We need to be very careful who we are talking about. *Josephine Feehily, chairperson, Revenue Commissioners.*

Cornycopia

All I was ever getting in the Dáil was for more money to be spent on education, for third level, for research, for cancer. I was never asked a question about the economy. Nobody cared a damn. I must have been the only prime minister in Europe that was hardly ever asked about the economy. It was just 'Spend more money, spend more money.' *Former Taoiseach Bertie Ahern.*

Guilt edged

It probably comes down to a mistake I made in buying shares, but that's where it lands ... When you're laid off because the chairman, Seán Quinn, lost €3 billion in shares, it's tough. *Seán Quinn, founder of the Quinn Group.*

A LITTLE LEARNING

These latest figures highlight that children who attend Irish-medium schools are in fact outperforming their English-medium counterparts in the two most important aspects of the primary curriculum—English and maths. The assessment figures indicate that children in Gaelic-medium education do better than children from similar socio-economic backgrounds who attend English-medium schools. *Dr Réamaí Mathers, Comhairle na Gaelscolaíochta, on recent Northern Ireland research.*

Flushed with success

There's such pressure to get the required CAO points that students will take all kinds of risks, and a lot of them believe they can get away with it because in many cases it is very difficult to prove that they are cheating ... The cheating ranges from something as unsophisticated as looking over someone else's shoulder and copying their answers to taking one of several toilet breaks and checking answers on their internet-enabled phones. *Maths teacher Brendan Gildea on Leaving Cert cheating.*

Twinkling little stars

I was teaching before and I was a jolly good teacher. I would do it again, but, God forgive me for my lack of tolerance, I would take only extremely talented children. I wouldn't have time for the plodders in my life. I would take only the gifted ones and give master classes to them alone. *Actress and entertainer Adele King (Twink).*

School's out

I will lock every classroom, put the alarm on and close over the gate. I have lovely memories here. I loved school when I was here and I loved my job. It is the end of an era. *Caretaker Valerie O'Hare as St John's Primary School, Glenn, Co. Down, closes as a result of falling numbers.*

This school provided education since 1921 as a boarding and day school for girls, and this work of Catholic education was very much the life work of the Benedictine community. Sadly, in more recent times, with the decline in vocations to the monastery, the managing of the boarding school became too great a workload, and consequently the decision to close was taken. *Principal Mary Dempsey, Kylemore Abbey, Co. Galway.*

FUN & GAMES

I would never have swapped the two years I was involved in the English setup. It was an amazing experience. What was difficult was I played seventeen games for England and two of them were against Ireland. If I could do it again, I would try to avoid playing those two games. *Cricketer Ed Joyce returns to the fold.*

Up for the Cup
What annoys me most about the World Cup is how the BBC coverage never shuts up about England. They keep harking back to 1966. *Peter Donegan, gardener, north Dublin.*

That very much depends on the pub. Perhaps there has been a softening in attitudes among the middle classes, but there is still a traditional hatred of the English among some people. I have been called a 'fucking English twat' in pubs, and I have had complete strangers come up to me to gloat if England lost a match. *Dublin-based journalist Maurice Newman, asked if he would wear an England shirt in a pub.*

I thought to myself, 'This could make or break me.' But I figured the risk was worth it after inspecting all the pitches over a week. It's been a challenge, but as an Irishman you'll always be keen to back the underdog, so we decided to go for it. *'Pitch doctor' Richard Hayden, hired by FIFA to ensure the highest standards at all the World Cup venues in South Africa.*

Out of the pram
We're only doing a job; it's minor league stuff in the bigger scheme of things, but you have to believe it's important—and it *is* important. We're not curing any sick patients, we're not splitting the atom, but if you start thinking in those terms you won't take your work seriously. Sports

journalism—it used to be called the toy department—well, it *is* the toy department, but we love toys. *Sports commentator Eamon Dunphy.*

Four!

It all started with his dad Gerry bringing Rory up to Holywood when he was a toddler, probably still in his nappies. Rory had plastic clubs and would chip around the lower putting green. He loved the game, it's all he ever wanted to do. *Rory McIlroy's coach Michael Bannon.*

Camán mate!

They can certainly adapt, they're big guys. They're very athletic and the eye-hand co-ordination is there. They were catching balls way up in the sky. It takes a bit of time, obviously, but there's not a million miles between both sports. *Hurler D. J. Carey puts the visiting Australian cricket team through their paces at Croke Park.*

AG OBAIR

It is very hard to be upbeat about things, because here in Northern Ireland it was a great place to be when the peace dividend started to kick in and the politicians started to act like real politicians, interested in things such as hospitals and schools. So while there were some good years for architects, this recession could not have come at a worse time for us. We are a resilient bunch, though. You will probably find that very few of those unemployed architects are signing on the dole. What they tend to do is to set up their own practices if they get laid off and try to get something going. *Frank McCloskey, Royal Society of Ulster Architects.*

Noblesse oblige

I'm driven by history. One can't not be when you sit at a dining table with your ancestors going directly back seven or eight generations, and they're all looking down at you, and being reared by my father, who'd maybe look at them and say, this one built the telescope, and that one built the suspension bridge, and this one invented the steam turbine, and this one invented photography, and then point a finger at me, say, and now, what are you going to invent? What are you going to contribute to keep the place afloat, it'll be your turn? *The Earl of Rosse, Birr Castle, Co. Offaly.*

Some people call the House of Lords a drop-in centre for the elderly, and we have to work against that perception. I can only speak for myself. I am here and I ask questions. I won't vote on small issues like the health affairs of Somerset because I don't know enough about that region and think it wouldn't be fair. But if there is a vote affecting Northern Ireland or a vote on large issues it is our responsibility to be there and make it count. *Lord Laird.*

Lost in translation

We find it hard to understand how the State can spend millions of euro per year on interpreting without any auditing of contracts or quality control. Members of our association, for example, have come across court interpreters who do not know the meaning of basic words such as 'guilty' or 'judge'. *Mary Phelan, Irish Translators' and Interpreters' Association.*

Any foreign national with a mobile phone and a notepad who speaks reasonable English can operate as an interpreter in a completely unregulated environment. *Detective Tom O'Sullivan, Garda Representative Association.*

CREATURES GREAT & SMALL

She was definitely stolen. I heard her screams at three in the morning, and by the time I got downstairs she was gone. Someone must know where she is. She shouts out her name a lot. I've set up a Facebook page to find her; I don't know what else to do. *Denise McGowan, Clonsilla, Dublin, on the loss of her parrot, Ruby.*

Hare raising

Hares may mistake the tall grass of silage fields as a good spot for lying up and giving birth. Silage is harvested during the peak period when leverets are born in late spring and early summer, and the machinery used may trap and kill young hares, driving local population declines year after year. Basically hares have fallen foul of an ecological trap. *Dr Neil Reid, Queen's University School of Biological Sciences.*

Within an inch of his life

It's very interesting. The male looks after the young, takes them on his back and will sometimes get a female to lay unfertilised eggs to feed his tadpoles. Poison dart frogs try to drown one another when they fight, and this can happen in as little as an inch of water. *Ian Millichip, Herpetological Society of Ireland, on his study of a rare South American breed.*

FAREWELL TO ARM

I can't feel my arm—I think the blood circulation's been cut off. I wrote about twelve-and-a-half pages. *Lee Bird, Glasnevin, Dublin, in the wake of the Leaving Certificate English 2 paper.*

Green people want to close the zoo

—want to stop horseracing,' claims expelled Fianna Fáil TD Mattie McGrath during the course of the contentious debates on bills to ban stag-hunting and categorise canines: 'They want to stop the pussy cat going after the mouse. To use their logic they want us to shut up shop and go home, eat lettuce and listen to Bob Geldof.' The bills are, nevertheless, passed.

No one thought about what would happen to the deer herd or the stag hounds before the ban was introduced. In fact, nothing about this ban was thought out. Some politicians asked John Gormley what he intended to do about the animals, and he just shook his head and said nothing. *Christy Reynolds, chairman, Ward Union Hunt.*

The stag is not killed. That is not the purpose of what we do. The stag is released and then it is chased and caught and brought back to the deer reservation. Sometimes, the stag escaped completely. I have only been on one hunt where the stag died, and that was accidental. *Joanne Quirke, member, Ward Union Hunt.*

How would Deputy Tuffy like it if I chased her pet beagle around the road or gave it a good kick up the rear end and scared the living bejasus out of it? What if I then told her that her animal would recover in a few days but that I got a great laugh out of it, and sure is that not sport? *Green Party TD Paul Gogarty during the wildlife debate.*

Most people who join the Labour Party are people of conviction. I am opposed to stag-hunting and I believe it to be wrong. I couldn't have voted against the ban. I and others had signed petitions opposing stag-hunting, so I had to stick to my word. *Deputy Tommy Bruen, expelled from the parliamentary party for his refusal to oppose the Bill.*

The Minister will have to give a guarantee on the floor of the House that this Bill and the Bill to be taken next week will be the end of his ramblings in rural Ireland. *Mary O'Rourke TD believes that Limerick native John Gormley should confine himself to the capital.*

Eaves droppings

People do not realise that carrying out work on their roof spaces at this time of the year could spell doom for a maternity roost. Bats like roofs because they are safe places for them to raise their babies. Each bat has only one pup, and it is heartbreaking to think that mother and child could end up being destroyed due to negligent or irresponsible behaviour on our part. *Robin Moffit, Bat Group, Partnership Against Wildlife Crime in Northern Ireland.*

Anybody here seen Kelli?

These birds get stressed very easily when taken out of their environment. They don't react well to it and it could have caused a heart attack. They don't deal well with being handled ... She was panting a little. Her mate was also panting and would have been more stressed because he had been left alone. They bond together very strongly. *Dublin Zoo keeper Eddie O'Brien on the kidnapping of Kelli, a Humboldt penguin, found wandering the streets of the city.*

Born and bread

When we were young, if we wasted any bread my dad would have gave us a clip round the ear. We were told to chop up the bread and give it out to the birds, and that hasn't stopped. How do you classify feeding wildlife as anti-social behaviour? *Gabby Curran, threatened with a £1,000 fine by Newry and Mourne District Council for feeding the birds.*

ARTS & PARTS

We certainly thought we would get more pictures going on the market than we have, because a painting is a reasonable liquid asset—if you need to sell a painting, you can put it on the market and it will find its level and sell relatively quickly. We haven't had that. In fact, we have had very few instances of people saying, 'Sell this for whatever you can get because we need the money.' *Rory Guthrie, de Veres art dealers.*

Verse and worse

Some might say that the writing of poems is other-worldly or something; it is and it isn't. There is something mysterious and outside normal activity, I accept that about the writing of poems, the making of art, but the root of good art will always be in the ordinary world, so it's not something completely detached or separate. There is the mundane, which is material, and there is the mysterious which is the flower of art which comes from ordinary life. I feel very much that I lead a practical life. It's not all up in the clouds stuff, the feet are on the ground, very firmly. *Poet, farmer and publisher Peter Fallon.*

There's too much 'Po-Biz' as they call it in the United States. The whole globalised creative writing racket. Poetry as a business. What I'm really trying to say is that you shouldn't be writing for a global audience. There should be a privacy and a measure of mystique to the work. Because it's a special activity, poetry. There are things we don't understand, philosophical things. I think of poetry as connecting with those things. Ideally. Maybe. Which implies a kind of inaccessibility or maybe inscrutability, ineffability on the part of the readers. Some word like that. *Poet Derek Mahon.*

The French poets to me seemed to be so dangerous, spending their time drinking absinthe and having riotous private lives. I was convinced I was going to be a Co. Tyrone Rimbaud. I've calmed down since. *Poet John Montague, on learning that he is to become a Chevalier de la Légion d'Honneur.*

Urban scrawl

Dublin has been awarded this accolade because of the rich historical literary past of the city, the vibrant contemporary literature, the variety of festivals and attractions available and because it is the birthplace and home of literary greats. *Minister for Tourism Mary Hanafin on the city's being named a UNESCO City of Culture.*

I guess Dublin must be very proud of its writers, because they have a whole room of them in the Wax Museum, where we also went, even though I've never heard of any of them. I thought Seán O'Casey was the name of a bridge until I saw a poster advertising one of his plays. Dublin could do a better job of telling us who these writers are. *Maryann Harmon, Denver, Colorado, interviewed outside the Long Room, TCD.*

If I had to choose between being the author of *Ulysses* or the Lord Mayor of Dublin, I would always choose to be the Lord Mayor of Dublin. *Gerry Breen, Lord Mayor of Dublin.*

DE MORTUIS

They say every genius is bordering on mad, and Alex was certainly that. You never knew if he would jump into the crowd or hit the referee or walk out. But he was also a fantastic cueman and played some great stuff. He created shots that everybody now copies. *Willie Thorne. Former world snooker champion Alex Higgins died this month.*

To people in the game he was a constant source of argument, he was a rebel. But to the wider public he was a breath of fresh air that drew them into the game. He was an inspiration to my generation to take the game up. I do not think his contribution to snooker can be underestimated. *Six times world champion Steve Davis.*

He mitched school, played snooker. A real good snooker player. Ten tables were in the Jampot Club. He played the top table. He was so good. *Boyhood friend Bobby Cummings, Belfast.*

He was a legend. It was him that made the game. I would never have watched otherwise. There's no airport to name after him now, so he should get a statue and a funeral like George Best had. *Joan Hanna, Belfast.*

LAW & DISORDER

We have never seen anybody sent to jail. Incarceration, in practical terms, does not happen in company law. *Kevin Prendergast, Office of the Director of Corporate Enforcement, on white-collar crime.*

As you were?

Nobody in Northern Ireland who has more than two brain cells to rub together wants to go back to the bad old days of the past, and I think we need to treat as pariahs those who would seek to take us there. *First Minister Peter Robinson on rioting in Belfast.*

There are still Neanderthals within our society who believe it's sensible to be involved in ongoing confrontation. *Deputy First Minister Martin McGuinness.*

There are individual politicians working very hard on this, but are we seeing the joined-up government? Are we seeing this, this morning, after a very difficult night, very damaging for Northern Ireland, these images beamed across the United Kingdom and perhaps wider? Are we seeing the First Minister and the Deputy First Minister stepping out to condemn this? I haven't heard from them. *Assistant Chief Constable Alastair Finlay.*

I saw a fellow approach carrying a five-gallon can of diesel in a clear container—I could see the red colour. I was shouting at him, 'There's women and children on this train, and you will kill them.' He looked at me and said, 'Fuck them. Let 'em burn.' *A Good Samaritan, anonymous for his own safety, tries to intervene in an attempt by local thugs to set fire to the Belfast–Dublin train at Lurgan, Co. Armagh.*

We know that more than half a million people enjoy the Twelfth, and there is hard evidence that an increasing number of tourists are planning trips to Northern Ireland at that time of year so they can see the parades. *David Hume, Orange Order.*

Room service

Tipstaffs and sitting room allowances seem like a throwback to the Victorian era. A tipstaff just ushers a judge into his chambers, drives his car, etc.—it's like something out of the 19th century. At a time when people are experiencing cutbacks, this is a luxury judges can do without. *Bernard Allen, chairman, Dáil Public Accounts Committee.*

Off with his head!

The allegation was one of perjury, which means I deliberately and knowingly gave an untrue version of accounts in an affidavit. I knew I hadn't done that. But I still lost my job. It's like something out of *Alice in Wonderland*: pass the sentence now and have the trial later. *Former minister Willie O'Dea, on being told he had no criminal case to answer.*

MEEJA

In 1996, I had to go for a Secret Service investigation to get my White House press pass. Only 10 years previously I'd been spending every Saturday afternoon hurling abuse at the American embassy, but it didn't stop me. Either the investigation wasn't that good or they overlooked my childhood indiscretions. *Former RTÉ Washington correspondent and student protester Mark Little.*

Up front
There is an element of trial and error in finding out who attracts readers. But Irish women seem to like people who they feel an affinity with. They like strong, bright Irish women. Colette Fitzpatrick has worked well for us in the past, and I think Lorraine Keane is maybe the only person we've had on two covers. The presentation of them as smiling, approachable and not super-intimidating is attractive. Irish Tatler *editor Jessie Collins.*

As seen on TV
When an individual has a programme or media platform and then is involved in that kind of advertising, it undermines public confidence in both the product and the person. The same person cannot be seen to be advertising a brand, only then to present a show. It will eventually have a corrosive effect on the media, and the public will find it unpalatable and tasteless and will not tolerate it. *Colum Kenny, School of Communications, Dublin City University.*

BRICKS & MORTAR

There is no property ladder any more. People want homes they can live in rather than investments. They're thinking if they're going to have a mortgage around their necks they want to have it on a house they can live in to a ripe old age. That's why these well-established suburbs close to the city centre with good amenities and public transport are doing well. *Market analyst Paul O'Connor.*

Fringe benefits
Social history tends to construct Irish people as rural or urban, but the major transformation is that most now live in suburban areas. No one has

ever really looked at these communities. *Sociology professor Mary Corcoran, NUI Maynooth.*

Life in the suburbs is all pros and no cons. In the country, people live in each other's pockets and everyone knows your business, and there's too much crime in the city centre. *John Jennings, Firhouse, Co. Dublin.*

A la tart

The house was bought in the 1960s, as I understand it, by a brothel keeper from Dublin, to entertain his favourite clients in the countryside. So it's the only farmhouse in the whole region with an en-suite bathroom for every bedroom and a bar and dancefloor downstairs. *Writer DBC Pierre on his Co. Leitrim residence.*

CHURCH & STATE

Take the list of names that he calls himself. The Roman Catholic Church turns to us and says you shouldn't call him the anti-Christ. Well, if a man comes to me and says he can forgive sins, then he is taking the place of Christ—no one can forgive sins except God. A person like some of the priests we've had destroying the lives of young people and then going out and saying I can forgive sins—it's only right that he be called what he is. That is anti-Christ in teaching and in doctrine. *Rev. Ian Paisley reverts to form.*

Passportout

Ireland is like Canada or Australia. It is considered a useful country for intelligence services—the Russians, Israelis and others—to use. You don't have to come up with an elaborate cover for proof of residence there. It keeps you away from all the troubles of using an American passport, which gets you more scrutiny. It's a fairly easy cover to put together. *Former CIA officer Bruce Riedel on Irish passports faked by a Russian spy network.*

Ireland isn't seen as some sort of state of grace on the edge of Europe. A lot of people have no real knowledge about who we are aligned to, or not, although there is a general awareness that we are part of the Western community of nations. What makes the Irish passport attractive is not the notion of neutrality. People of our ethnicity live in English-speaking countries all over the world, and an awful lot qualify for an Irish passport. So you can be an Irish passport-holder and not need to sound as though you come from Co. Clare. *Security and defence analyst Declan Power.*

The technology we now have in place in terms of the Irish passport system is of a very high specification. But you will know from listening to people in the technology world and elsewhere, the capacity of certain organisations out there to almost penetrate any technology is well known. *Minister for Foreign Affairs Mícheál Martin.*

The heart's a wonder
After Camillus died in 1614, they did an autopsy on him. They felt his heart was somewhat magnificent because of the life he led. They took it out and it's remained uncorrupted ever since. We do nothing to preserve it and it's stood the test of time, which we see as a providential sign. *Fr Stephen Foster, Order of St Camillus, on the arrival of the saint's relic in Ireland.*

For the good of their health
There's a huge issue around the excessive secrecy and legalism of the HSE, and it strikes me that it is a cultural thing within the HSE. And it is redolent of a body that looks not to the public interest, which is the only reason it's there, and seeks instead to protect its own interests, and that's very wrong. *Ombudsman Emily O'Reilly.*

Take it from here
Once the State makes something legal, people automatically think it is okay for them. That is why the introduction of divorce has such a negative effect on our understanding of marriage. People think that if the State sees nothing wrong with the law then it is morally right. That is how new laws can change the perceptions of people. *Bishop of Elphin Christopher Jones on the Civil Partnership Bill.*

HERE & THERE

Kildare was an army town. Soldiers and jockeys, and I always thought it was quite cosmopolitan, oddly, because you had all these soldiers and jockeys coming from Dublin and all over. *Presenter and Kildare native Ray D'Arcy.*

Into Africa

I remember the excitement before we left. None of us had ever been near an airport, not to mind an airplane. I was part of the engineering corps and did carpentry, but I did a lot of duties like patrolling the border between the Congo and Rwanda. Our main task was to keep the airport open over there—it was the only way in and out of the country. I look back on it now as a fantastic achievement. *Corporal Patrick Clancy, Youghal, Co. Cork, recalling the army's first UN mission, to the Congo, on its fiftieth anniversary.*

The captain announced what had happened—and you've never seen so many rosary beads and scapulars appearing. The Irish mammies had given rosary beads to every young soldier. They all appeared—by the dozen! *Jim Carton, Wexford, on the aircraft losing one of its engines on the flight over.*

We had arrived in 'bull's wool' uniforms, which were far too hot. We got the tropical gear, but the problem was it was never measured. My trousers were trailing on the ground and reached up to my chest. Then I had green, white and gold braces, which could barely reach over my shoulder. It might as well have been a clown's costume. *Godfrey Ledger, Limerick.*

The most dramatic moment was winning the battle of 'the tunnel' on the outskirts of Elizabethville [Lubumbashi]. We were being fired on from all sides—it was our first time under fire. I was scared—who wouldn't be? I think I appreciated life much more after that. *Sergeant Noel McGivern, Dublin.*

The Queen's shilling

I didn't want the Irish army—not busy enough. The French Foreign Legion sent on the package of information, but I threw it out. I was originally going to join the Paras, but I was told about the Royal Irish. Some people don't care that I joined; other people don't talk about it. Some of the guys in Ruislip weren't happy about it. Some of the family haven't found out yet. *Seán Ryan, Kilmaley, Co. Clare, British soldier and sometime employee of Robert Emmets hurling club, Ruislip, Middlesex.*

Liquid assets

The last pirates on the Shannon were the Danes. They came from Dublin—ironically—round the coast, up through Limerick, and all they took were the ecclesiastical artefacts and the occasional fed-up nun. And their entire escapades were brought to a conclusion under the terms of the first Good Friday Agreement at Clontarf, courtesy of Brian Bórú. In the intervening 1,000 years, we've had no raiding party on the Shannon—until now, and, ironically, the pirates emanate from the same source and will be repudiated with the same force. *Veteran campaigner P. J. Walsh on the proposal to pipe water in quantity from Lough Derg to the capital.*

SOCIAL & PERSONAL

Please, please live life on its terms, within its rules and boundaries; otherwise life will be cruel and merciless towards you and towards the family and friends who will have to bear you to the grave. *Fr John Walsh, at the funeral of some of the victims of the Co. Donegal car crash in which eight people died—the worst such incident since records began.*

Bien Aimé

Nobody of that fame has come around here before. I'm still amazed they picked it, but it's great for the place and everyone extends a welcome to them. *Pat Kilkenny, Mohill, Co. Leitrim, on the choice of Aughavas, Mohill, for the wedding of actress Amy Huberman and Ireland rugby captain Brian O'Driscoll.*

It's lifted the county. There has been no recession in Leitrim for the last three weeks while locals have been preparing for this. *Clement Gaffney, Lough Rynn Castle, hosting the wedding reception.*

I thanked him for taking the bruises for us and gave his muscles a stroke. I told him they should parade down the town after the wedding, but he said it wasn't in the plan, unfortunately. *Maureen Lynch, Mohill.*

Shortt shrift

I've got a trainer, but I don't go to him enough, and the same man wouldn't even want his name associated with me because I'm not the best advertisement for him, the poor old divil. I've been with him a year now and he's fantastic. He beats me into submission. He's worse than a dominatrix. Then I go off on tour, and a week or two lapses, and then I'm back to him again; I go to him for a couple of weeks and I lose a bit of weight and I'm all fit and drinking juices and talking shite, and then I go to the pub. *Entertainer Pat Shortt.*

Foot in the door

It all goes back to 1858 when the shoemaker in Enniskerry tried to kill his wife but ended up stabbing her brother instead. Wicklow Jail was where he ended up, and that left a vacancy for a shoemaker in Enniskerry. Enter Terry's ancestor, Michael Wogan, a bootmaker from Dublin, who got the job. *Historian Brian White, researching the genealogy of radio and TV presenter Terry Wogan.*

AG OBAIR

I have really found in recent months that there are people out there just waiting for you to trip up. They are like cats waiting to pounce. I don't want that for the rest of my life. I know it's obvious in any profession, but it's a particular feature of the modelling and showbiz industry. *Model Rosanna Davison contemplates a career change.*

Coal comfort

You might have only an old shirt and pants. There was no such thing as oilskins. Or gloves. There wasn't even a piecebox to carry your lunch; you'd carry your lunch in a bit of paper. And try to hide that from the rats. Umpteen times they'd get it. *Former miner Jim O'Neill on life on the Castlecomer coalfield, Co. Kilkenny.*

Casing the joint

The worst summer job I had was in a factory in Normandy that made false knee caps and hip replacements. My job was in Quality Control. I was on a conveyor belt, picking up knees, looking for tiny black specks, except somebody had already checked them. I was the double-checker for black spots. *Comedian Dermot Whelan.*

PARTY LINES

Deputy Gilmore, if I may be excused the analogy, reminds me of a gadfly around the tail of an old cow. He circles, you don't hear him; sometimes he might land, but you don't see him land; but all the time you know he is there and you know that in the final analysis you will never quite know what he is up to, where he is going, or how he is going to get there. *Former Ceann Comhairle John O'Donoghue TD on the Labour Party leader.*

Giving way to tentation
There can be no room in Fine Gael for cute-hoor politics. We cannot on the one hand condemn Fianna Fáil for entertaining developers in the Galway tent while on the other hand extending the biscuit tin for contributions from high-profile developers who are beholden to NAMA. *Fine Gael TD Lucinda Creighton.*

Fine Gael have no truck with rogue builders, with hooky characters or shady characters. We have no dealing with brown envelopes, influence-buying or dig-outs. The party is absolutely above board in all its financial dealings. *Party leader Enda Kenny.*

Going with the flow
The River Boyne will flow backwards before Noel Dempsey builds the Navan line. *Fine Gael TD Damien English doubts the Minister for Transport's assertion that the restoration of the railway will go ahead despite announced cutbacks.*

FUN & GAMES

It was well worked and it was a definite goal. People are saying I threw it in, but I was heading for the line, and I just dropped the ball and it was in the net. I got it and the lad just pushed me into the net. I tried to do whatever I could to hit it, and the goal was given, simple as that. *Meath captain Joe Sheridan, scorer of the hotly disputed goal with which Meath defeated Louth in the last minute of extra time.*

It seems to be always the small teams that get screwed with these sorts of decisions. It wouldn't happen to Meath, it wouldn't happen to Dublin, it wouldn't happen to Kerry. *Louth captain Paddy Keenan.*

It's just very unfortunate that it happens in a high-profile game right at the end of a game to a team that hasn't won in a long time. It's just a very unfortunate situation. *Meath captain Nigel Crawford.*

The treatment of the referee was absolutely disgraceful. We will need a serious review of our security at Croke Park. A course of action might need to be taken against individuals that transgressed security. *GAA president Christy Cooney.*

Wolves supporter

Sure what woman wouldn't want to be whistled at? It's a compliment. That's how I met my wife, by whistling at her. She got the short straw, because I've been married to her for twenty-four years. *Joe Mahon, Irvinestown, Co. Fermanagh, organiser of the World Wolf-Whistling Contest.*

I got roped in today for some unknown reason. I didn't realise I was going to show as much leg as I did. If I'd known that I probably would have declined. But sure it was all a bit of craic. *Marion Richardson, persuaded to run the whistlers' gauntlet.*

Lycanthropy rules OK

They tell me I'm a world champion now, but I've no free holiday out of it yet. *Butcher and winning wolf-whistler Stephen Miller, Irvinestown.*

Give it a whirl!

Will I be going up on it? I certainly will not. I hate heights and have vertigo. Maybe I could be convinced, if I could find a couple of very beautiful women to come with me. *Property developer Harry Crosbie, installer of Dublin's big wheel.*

CÓRAS IOMPAIR

After the disaster in April 1912, *Titanic* wasn't talked about because there was a sense of shame, but with the discovery of the wreck in 1985 that changed. There was a renewed awareness in the story and a pride in the Belfast shipyard. I felt if our tourist industry was to involve the ship someone with a genuine interest and a personal story should be involved, so I left my reporting career with UTV in 2008 to develop this idea, and it has mushroomed. *Susie Millar, whose great-grandfather went down with the ship, now running Titanic Tours Belfast.*

De profundis

We wanted something for the National Maritime Museum to keep the memory of this vessel alive, and all it stood for. The government fed us with lies and delaying tactics on the future of the ship and of sail training after the sinking, and then cancelled the whole programme. *Captain Gerry Burns, former master of the sail trainer* Asgard, *on an unauthorised dive on the wreck.*

How would Coiste an Asgard feel if the ship's bell was hanging in some French bar, because it is open season for any diving team? I have letters from former defence minister Willie O'Dea, and I've had correspondence with Coiste an Asgard, and it was fully aware of our intentions and didn't have the courage to stop us. *Deep-sea diver Eoin McGarry, leader of the dive that recovered the relics.*

He took it for a test drive himself. He came back and said to me there was something wrong with the reverse gear. I thought maybe he is just not used to putting it into reverse gear, so I went out with him on a test drive. We pulled up on the pier, and I showed the man how the car operated in reverse … and he agreed it was fine. Before I knew it, he'd put the car into forward and sped up and driven off the edge of the pier … Within, I'd say, ten to fifteen seconds the whole car was submerged. *Jeremy Beshoff, Beshoff Motors, Howth, Co. Dublin, who broke a window and surfaced unharmed. The driver perished.*

Joined-up thinking

Our strategy is to connect Ireland to the world. We bring passengers from New Zealand to Ireland and from Ireland to Argentina. All that is possible with Aer Lingus, with us and our partners. *Chief executive Christoph Müller.*

Tunnel vision

It's a very significant undertaking. It's eighteen kilometres long and there will be a lot of complex work in the city centre. It compares very well with Vancouver, which is just opened. It's uncannily similar in terms of length and numbers of stations, and they have the same sort of constraints that we have here. *Project manager Rob Leech on plans for Dublin's Metro North.*

Sizing up

We have a very small, efficient fleet which manages one of the largest maritime spaces in the European Union. Side by side with that, compared to the naval arms of the other member-states in the European Union, we are very sleek and very efficient. But those who go down to the ships at sea deserve to be in modern ships. We cannot allow the naval service to go back to the bad old days of the forties and fifties where they struggled around with a few corvettes. *Minister for Finance Brian Lenihan, announcing two new vessels for the Naval Service.*

Armchair traveller

The first thing I noticed when I got to Sligo was the cosy train station—it felt like I was in somebody's living room. *Katarina Korenova, Slovakian visitor to the Yeats International Summer School.*

'ATIN' & DRINKIN'

I think having a music festival with no alcohol is brave; it's bold and it's innovative. But it'll take a long time to work. The big stigma against it is that Irish people find it impossible to socialise without alcohol. *David McGoldrick, manager, The Whatmans, on Sligo's sparsely attended Lovin' Life Festival.*

Calling the shots

It is disgusting that IRA car bombs, which killed and maimed so many in Northern Ireland, are being trivialised or celebrated in this way. I would have expected Americans, of all people, to behave more sensitively and responsibly. How would they like it if we developed the al-Qaeda car bomb, the Twin Towers cocktail, or the 9/11 ice-cream sundae? *Willie Frazer, IRA victims' group FAIR, on the promotion of an 'Irish Car Bomb' cocktail (Guinness, Bailey's, whiskey) in American bars.*

Bombe surprise

There was a specific moment when I stood up one day in the kitchen, and I looked around and watched the others working, and I could see the world around me. It was an epiphany. I smiled to myself: 'I get it now. I see how it's done.' I realised there was a career here. *Cathal Armstrong, Killiney, Co. Dublin, owner of the four-star restaurant Eve, Virginia, USA.*

VE HAVE VAYS ...

German women must have ways of extracting money from foolish Irishmen that Irish women have not been able to accomplish yet. *Judge Mary Fahy on the case of a German woman accused of robbing an Irish boyfriend.*

I lost two stone without even trying

—says former TD Mildred Fox on her decision to leave politics: 'There was much less time driving around, sitting at meetings and grabbing meals.' Her departure, however, served to further reduce both the number and the percentage of women TDs, a situation that moves several of their limited residue to call for a quota system. Not all, however, are of the same mind.

In an ideal world I wouldn't agree with it—if there was better participation of women in politics. But given the situation as it is, I just think it is necessary just to allow women to break through the ranks of the political party structures and to be represented on the ticket. *Beverley Flynn TD.*

I don't believe quotas are a solution to gender imbalance in the Oireachtas or politics generally. The lifestyle is very unappealing to women, as is the culture within the political parties. Introducing quotas is a very easy way to get people off the hook … I don't want to sound sexist in reverse! *Lucinda Creighton TD.*

This 'I'm all right, Jill' shows a sad lack of solidarity with other women. *Susan McKay, National Women's Council, on those opposing quotas.*

Back in 2002, I think it was estimated that it would take 360 years for women to achieve equal representation in Irish politics, but given that the proportion of women in politics has decreased since then, it's going to take even longer. *Dr Sandra McAvoy, UCC.*

HIS & HERS

I remember thinking: 'I'm the only lesbian in Mount Merrion, and no one will ever love me.' *Novelist Emma Donoghue.*

Kneejerk reaction

Imagine sitting in a nightclub where women push you out of the way like you're a piece of dirt to try and sit on your husband's knee. It's not in my character to put up with that. I'm a bit of a thunderous bitch when I have to be. *Gillian Quinn, wife of former Republic of Ireland soccer star Niall Quinn.*

Altar egos

I have seen ceremonies where two interpreters were required for a marriage when clearly the bride and groom couldn't understand each other. Other indicators are: a man holding all the documents for a woman; the bride and groom not knowing each other's address at the interview; a bride having no friend at a ceremony; and the same people often attending different marriages. *HSE Superintendent Registrar Dennis Prior on the incidence of sham marriages.*

Open invitation

Of all my former classmates in Poland, I am probably one of only three people not married, and I am only twenty-four. Irishmen are more into parties and a see-how-it-goes approach. They are more fun. One thing, though, I notice the manners are different. Polish guys always open the door first. That's not the same with some Irish guys. *Fabiola Galeziewska.*

Blow-dry

In Australia, men are more conscious about their hair and clothing. You only have to look at the mixed-rules series every year to see the difference between the Australian males and the Irish. Here, some of the GAA lads look like they've been hit with a hurley a few times too many. Some Irish men still look like little boys when they grow up … You see almost helpless men who have been raised by their mammy until they are forty or fifty. I wouldn't like to be marrying any man who had that. *Australian Lisa Domican, Greystones, Co. Wicklow.*

Sexplanations

It's astonishing how many Irish people don't have an understanding of their own sexual functions. The lack of education in this area is huge. Men don't understand the pace of arousal for women. It's much slower than a man's, and this is something that often creates difficulty. Added to which, quite a lot of people are still uncomfortable with, and have scant knowledge of, their own bodies. Some people are appalled about the idea of pleasure. *Sex therapist Eithne Bacuzzi.*

Ballybrack, south Dublin, a laneway in the late 1970s near where I grew up. There were two fellas sitting on top of the wall, and I started talking to them; then they just came out with it, just like that, very matter of fact: 'This is what happens when a man and woman go to bed.' Decades later people ring up my radio show with some shocking stories, but nothing can match my shock back then. *Presenter Adrian Kennedy.*

When I was six my mate in school told me that his dad magically made a baby by putting himself between his wife's legs. As a kid I thought, How could any magic happen with all the clothes and aprons in the way? *Comedian Brendan Burke.*

Three score years and then ...

If you behave as if you're seventy, you're done for. *Lady Miranda Iveagh, celebrating her seventieth birthday.*

FADÓ, FADÓ

Staircases are the key to Skellig Michael's historical chronology, since the sixth century or further back and up until the period when the Commissioners of Irish Lights would also have created access routes. The different staircases may indicate a far more complex pattern of settlement than previously documented, or they may also indicate a far more daring pilgrimage circuit was created on the island, at a time when it was a pilgrimage site. *Archaeologist Michael Gibbons.*

No place like Rome

I've always had an interest in history, but, basically, if I'm honest, the movie *Gladiator* did it for me. I went to watch it, and I thought it looked like fun;

next thing I know, I see an advertisement in a window saying a Roman group is forming. And that was that ... We do everything like the Romans would have. If we didn't, it would be like the equivalent of buying football boots but not playing the game. *Shane Kent, at a military show and Roman re-enactment in Cork City Jail.*

Many things I have seen here you cannot show in Germany. It is very dangerous to show this in our country, and the police come and get you. It is a little bit shocking to see it here, to be honest. *Udo Henka on the representation of Nazi-era memorabilia at the Cork military show.*

MAMMON

An Irish version of market totalitarianism is a domestic McCarthyism where every sector of Irish society is subject to the cost-benefit rationale as demonstrated by the recent McCarthy report and the planned deliberations over the sale of State assets. The result is that human beings are seen as purely instrumental means to economic ends and if they are not fit for economic purpose they are considered valueless. *Professor Michael Cronin, Dublin City University.*

All to play for
These houses were built as playpens for the rich to lavish money on. Today it's the opposite: we all have to find ways to make them pay for themselves. It comes down to how much you're willing to sacrifice in terms of privacy and lifestyle. It takes a lot of dosh—and a strategy. *John Cosby of Stradbally Hall (1563) on the sustainability of heritage houses.*

Tenable position?
We looked at leaders worldwide who are facing tough economic and political environments, many of whom are making unpopular decisions, both fiscally and socially. While many of the measures that world leaders are taking right now are indeed controversial, some countries seem better poised to bounce back in the long run, and Ireland qualified for that criteria. *Jan Angilella, Newsweek (New York), on the magazine's nomination of Brian Cowen as one of the world's top ten leaders.*

CREATURES GREAT & SMALL

I had two cows for showing, and I brought the calf as well for a competition for calves, but it went missing from the marquee some time between 7.30 p.m. and 8 p.m. that evening. I am appealing for its return, because calves are like dreams, and this one was going to be a wonderful animal, and I have her grandmother. *Cattle-breeder Ivan Robinson, Ballygowan, Co. Down, on a bad experience at Virginia Show, Co. Cavan.*

Favouring the bowlers

Mongrels, crosses, they're all welcome here. When I'm judging, it's a case of something catching my eye, whether it's the appearance of a dog or the way it carries itself. Some dogs have a certain quality to them that keeps drawing your eye back. Those are the dogs that I'm picking as winners today. *John McCullough, judge at Scruffts Dog Show, Moy, Co. Armagh.*

Dogs have a universal draw—everyone loves them. I came in to make one dog, and I just kept going. There was a great sense of completion about getting a dog finished. *Filmmaker Mars O'Reilly on her contribution to the 120 papier-mâché pooches—created as part of the Cork Dog Project.*

Knocking-bird thrill

It's the first time a forest bird like this has colonised in Ireland. Everybody should be excited about it. They are gorgeous creatures, and they are very beautiful and intelligent to watch. The sound of them on a tree is amazing. On a clear day you can hear it up to a mile away. *Nigel Hatch, Birdwatch Ireland, on the first appearance (off the silver screen) of the great spotted woodpecker.*

Arch enemies

This is like a McDonald's for rats, and sooner or later the rats might decide there are better pickings to be had further afield in bins beside private houses. *Joe Friel, Clean Air Naas, on a closed waste facility at Kerdiffstown, Co. Kildare.*

P-peck up a pinguin

They may be cute-looking, but not by nature. They are fiercely aggressive when it comes to defending what is theirs. They have got a habit of rotating their neck when you walk up to the nest. I heard an American researcher say that they are trying to triangulate to peck your eyes out. It's not just that they are aggressive towards humans, they are aggressive towards each other, with a peck here and a peck there. *Keeper Garth de Jong, in charge of Dublin Zoo's Humboldt penguins.*

PARTY LINES

I do not see why a Fianna Fáil minister like Brian Lenihan, whose predecessors murdered Michael Collins, should be making the oration at the Michael Collins commemoration at Béal na Blath ... The Michael Collins commemoration will give them an aura of acceptability they will only abuse. *Fine Gael senator Liam Twomey.*

I don't imagine a Fine Gael person would ever be asked to speak at a de Valera function and nor do I believe they should. I think this invitation is a sign of maturity. It is a recognition that Civil War politics shouldn't be part of our politics today. *Nora Owen, former Fine Gael minister and grandniece of Michael Collins.*

It is true that over time the painful divisions from which emerged the two largest political parties in the State have more or less entirely healed ... If today's commemoration can be seen as a further public act of historical reconciliation at one of Irish history's sacred places, then I will be proud to have played my part. *Minister for Finance Brian Lenihan at Béal na Blath.*

Northern enlightenment
Let's stop kidding ourselves. We are never going to believe in each other's versions of the truth. And I think it's about time that we moved on. *Ian Paisley (Jnr) MP.*

Right there, Michael?
I have no time for republicans. Sinn Féin have gone with homosexuals, they've gone with lesbians, they've gone with homosexuals adopting children. People like us are really looked down upon; Ireland has really never had an extreme right-wing political movement ... *Michael Quinn, Democratic Right Movement.*

Ha'penny place

€2.60? Sure what's that anyway? Big deal, big fucking deal. If the council paid me €2.60—jaysus, great stuff. I must look for more, because I didn't get enough then. *Councillor Des Foley on claiming expenses for an event in his home town.*

CÚRSAÍ SPÓIRT

I wish to see you for two or three reasons. First, you miss me. I wish also show you I am not dead. I live very well. *Ireland manager Giovanni Trapattoni addresses the media on his release from hospital following surgery.*

Own goal

The England manager at the time was Graham Taylor; he had bought me at Aston Villa. I came on at 1-0, and Graham Taylor looked at me to sort of say, 'I paid a lot of money for you, don't you go on and score against us,' and, of course, I did. That was my greatest goal, my greatest moment scoring against England. I just loved that. *Former Republic of Ireland international Tony Cascarino.*

Don't fence me in

We have been shocked by the level of hostility to something that's being done purely in the interests of public safety. It has come from certain commentators, members of the public and, indeed, some of our own officers. We're being accused of abandoning tradition. *GAA Director-General Paraic Duffy on the proposal to fence in Hill 16 at Croke Park for safety reasons.*

You have to think of the unthinkable. There are reasons there were recommendations not to have fences, and there's no way I'd ever ascribe to any arrangement where crowds are penned in and the best way of their escape is blocked, for any period of time. You manage people with people, not with a fence. *Phil Scranton, expert on stadium safety.*

Retreat to Moscow

My view is, I need a break from it. I've had my experience of Glasgow, and I do need a change ... Some fans there hate everything Celtic stands for and everything I stand for as an Irish Catholic playing for Celtic. *Republic of Ireland international Aiden McGeady on signing for Spartak Moscow.*

O'Limpiad

Three years ago, I was chatting to Chris Evans on BBC Radio 2. I happened to be training for the three-legged marathon record, which I broke here in the Mardyke with my running-partner, John Meade. Evans said: 'You should compile everything you do into one athletic sports meet,' and I said, 'Paddy Games,' and thus the idea was born … *Fermoy solicitor Colin Carroll.*

CRIME & PUNISHMENT

Identity parades are a very important safeguard and are recognised as such by courts in cases that rely on identification. The most important aspect is that a suspect's solicitor is there, so they can make sure the process is fair and spot when the other suspects in the line-up don't closely resemble their client, for instance. The judge has to point out that honest people can make mistakes in identifying people … *Criminal lawyer Michael Staines.*

Release mechanism

It is intolerable that a convicted rapist such as Larry Murphy can be released, having served only 10 years of a 15-year prison sentence for the savage rape and attempted murder of a woman. Remission is tied into the process of rehabilitation, but in this case all and any attempts at rehabilitation were dismissed. It is impossible to understand why automatic remission should apply in cases like this. *Charlie Flanagan TD.*

All I can say to them is I will not be having him here. Basically I just want to get back to a normal life. My kids are here for the last five weeks, prisoners in this house. No matter where you go, you're looking over your shoulder for media. I just don't want to live like that, and I can't live like that. *Larry Murphy's brother Tom.*

Too much hysteria is unhelpful. I am confident of the Garda management system in place to monitor him. People should have faith in the Gardaí to do their jobs. *Retired assistant Garda commissioner Martin Donnellan on Larry Murphy.*

Is someone who has been convicted of a criminal offence and has served his sentence always a criminal, and not entitled to basic human and civil rights? *Press Ombudsman John Horgan.*

ARTS & PARTS

I'm very pleased at Londonderry's success in becoming the UK's capital of culture. To anyone who disputes our Britishness, the answer's clearly now in that title. But there is a danger that continuing sectarianism will alienate the Protestant community from the win. Every stone that's aimed at a Protestant home, every window that's broken, every petrol bomb that's thrown, every assault on the Apprentice Boys' parade next Saturday, will lead to members of the unionist community retorting: 'Some capital of culture this is!' *East Derry MP Gregory Campbell.*

There was a huge political dimension to it. Birmingham, Norwich and Sheffield were never going to win; this is a pat on the back for Derry in what I feel is a benign but patronising indulgence of us. There is a feeling, How nice it is that 'tragic wee Derry' got an award. *Former member of the Northern Ireland Civil Rights Association Eamonn McCann.*

Let's just say that if Derry were an artist he would be living in an unheated, windowless garret, with the arse out of his trousers. So, yes, a few bob wouldn't harm us. *Derry journalist and author Garbhan Downey.*

Great gas
It's Oxegen for older people. My generation don't go to Punchestown, we go to Glenties. We don't wear coloured wellingtons and sleep in tents, but we do get a bowl of porridge in the morning, go for a walk with our zimmer frames out along the beach, and then go into a big room to listen to people delivering speeches. *Former Labour Party leader Pat Rabbitte on the MacGill Summer School.*

Guilty without charge
It was as if I had committed a crime and I did not know what the crime was. Maybe the crime was to do with the strangulation and the silencing at that time. *Edna O'Brien on the banning in Ireland of her first novel,* The Country Girls.

I can't believe it's the fiftieth anniversary of that book. It still reads as if it had been written yesterday, or as if it might be written tomorrow. I wish she'd come back and live amongst us again—God knows, we need all the colour and humour we can get. *Novelist John Banville.*

Appointment deferred

I'm very grateful to God for letting me live this long, or whoever is up in Heaven, saying, 'For God's sake don't let that woman up here yet. Give us a little bit more peace before she gets here.' *Actor Maureen O'Hara, celebrating her ninetieth birthday.*

Extra mural

I am a bit perturbed that anyone could be arrested for recreating art. I didn't understand the difference between expressing art on paper and the side of a building. *TCD lecturer Paul Horan, arrested for writing poetry on a Carlow pub wall.*

AG OBAIR

It feels wonderful to be the ambassador to Ireland. This is one of the things that President Obama also thinks—he said, 'That's a great job to get.' Compared to his, I would say that's true. *US Ambassador Dan Rooney.*

High finance

When you work as a pilot you are involved with flying. You are also dealing with administration. I might be processing expenses or dealing with the security at the base. I couldn't work all the time in an ordinary office. My office has to be at 40,000 feet. *Air Corps Lieutenant Vincent Haigney.*

Wine and ease

I can't remember how I got the job of doing secretarial work for Edna O'Brien in the early 1960s: I certainly didn't deserve it, as I was a hopelessly disorganised secretary. But Edna was kind, and she must have hired me out of kindness. As an employer she was easy and indulgent. She fed me cake and Burgundy, which I thought wonderful. *Author and journalist Mary Kenny.*

FAITH & MORALS

I belong to an organisation that seems caught in a time warp, run by old celibate men divorced from the realities of life, with a lonely priesthood struggling with the burden of celibacy, where rules and regulations have more weight than the original message of community and love. *Jennifer Sleeman on organising a one-day protest boycott of Mass.*

Dress codes

I started wearing hijab after I converted in 2004 at the age of eighteen ... It's not for every woman, but it makes me feel so much more secure. I think the reasoning behind it is just common sense. It is a form of protection. Everywhere you look these days it's all about sex, sex, sex, sex. Men are weaker ... They react to images more than we do. They just can't control themselves. *Amna Han, originally from Tallaght, Co. Dublin.*

For many it gives a sense of privacy. I think the secular world has really misunderstood niqab. For a Muslim woman the niqab is not a tool to lock herself out of the world and cut people off. Rather it empowers her to invite women she wishes into her world. *Dublin Muslim Jasmina Kid.*

Kings in check

Until the Copernican revolution, monarchs exercised absolute control over their subjects by divine right. But when the peoples of the world, informed by a new cosmology, put the divine right of kings into history's dustbin, they forgot to toss the divine right of popes into the garbage, too. I am not attacking our Catholic faith. I am talking about the special and corrosive tyranny that popes have been exercising over Catholics everywhere ... *Religion commentator Robert Blair Kaiser, addressing the Humbert Summer School.*

Clouds of glory

My idea of heaven is moving from one smoke-filled room to another. The only exercise I take is walking behind the coffins of friends who took exercise. *Actor Peter O'Toole.*

MEEJA

RTÉ is the civil service. It's a big building with all these people doing nothing. RTÉ should be sold off and the people running it sacked. *Impresario Louis Walsh.*

Orientation

My news agency is the first Chinese media organisation to set up a permanent office in Ireland. The intention to open this bureau is to increase our news-gathering capacity in Ireland and seek closer co-operation with Irish media. *Journalist Xiong Sihao.*

'ATIN' & DRINKIN'

We see young people who have drunk themselves unconscious, people injured in fights, and those hurt in accidents. Alcohol is the biggest drug we have, and as a nation we don't seem to be able to take it in moderation. It far outweighs all the other drug problems we see here. *Dr Cathal O'Donnell, A&E, Western Regional Hospitals.*

Mint with a hole

The customers came to eat my food for a special occasion. Once the recession kicked in, the star put people off. Nowhere else in the world was it like that—just in Ireland. It was like a bad word, having a star. And, inevitably, customer spend went. We all realised that Ireland wasn't as wealthy as we thought it was. *Dylan McGrath, formerly of Dublin's Michelin-star Mint restaurant.*

Pint taken

I have no Irish blood in me, but I do have lots of Irish beer in me. If you drink Guinness you got to pay your respects. For such a famous man it's kind of strange that his grave is not on any of the official tourist literature. *Doug Stein, Kansas City, visiting Uncle Arthur's neglected resting-place, Oughterard, Co. Kildare.*

Muck spreading

I have to say that, after all my years in the food business, I am delighted to see that the Irish palate has finally been broadened. There was a time when the Irish would have turned their noses up at 'foreign muck', but I am glad to see that has changed—for the most part. *Matthew Spalding, Kanum Thai Food and Noodle Bar, Dublin.*

TURFED OUT

We will be fighting it the whole way. We'll be cutting turf anyways. Just the same as people continued to use condoms, even though they were illegal. And continued to be a Jew in Nazi Germany. *Luke 'Ming' Flanagan, Turf Cutters and Contractors' Association, on a new law banning cutting on thirty-two bogs in Specific Areas of Conservation.*

If you cut turf by hand for four hundred years, you essentially cut the bog away. With the way people are talking at the moment, you'd think they weren't doing anything. But just looking at the air photographs of the peat bogs, you can see it's all been diced up. Like somebody cutting a block of cheese. A bog only grows 1 mm per year, so each 30 cm sod of turf that's cut vertically—that's three hundred years of bog growth. *Catherine O'Connell, Irish Peatlands Conservation Council.*

It is lovely when you go round the countryside in July and you see the tractors hauling the big rakes, the big piles of turf. There is something very traditional about it. And the smell of it is lovely. *Donal Clarke, author of a history of Bord na Móna.*

When you're going through life down where we are here, and we've seen nothing else only turf, we've known no other way. That's kind of the way it is. *Patrick Connolly, Ticknevin, Co. Kildare, organiser of the annual all-Ireland turf-cutting competition.*

You could go to the bog now and you wouldn't see anybody. You'd be all on your own. Going back years ago you'd see hares, you had grouse, all those things. In the mornings you'd hear the corncrake. It was lovely to hear them. But that's gone, you see. Burning bog, I blame it on that. They see the fires, and it's the time of year they would be nesting and all that. It vanished them. *Farmer Seamus Gallagher, Ballyhaunis, Co. Mayo.*

CÓRAS IOMPAIR

The Gardaí have better things to do than stop someone taking their kids to school. Who in the name of God is going to bat an eyelid at that sort of thing? Are the Gardaí going to set up checkpoints to stop people with golf clubs? *Minister John Gormley on the new laws on the use of commercial vehicles for private purposes.*

Off the rails

I just can't deal with commuting. A lot of people who live here are commuters. I just think not having the rail link makes it so difficult to go places. I've travelled around Europe, and it is just so much more efficient, and everything is on time. Whereas in Navan if you don't have a car you are in trouble. *Navan student Aoife Strahan.*

Transmoggification

The odd time you might see a dog run onto the DART, but it's just not a cat thing to do. The cat just sauntered on to the DART at Malahide and was sitting up on the seat. She seemed to befriend passengers on the journey, and a woman handed her over to staff at Pearse Station. *Iarnród Éireann spokesperson Barry Kenny on commuter cat Lilou, who received a Rail Smart Card for future use.*

DE MORTUIS

When I met Mick he was already a big star, and I was as star-struck as anybody, really. I was blown away by him. When I got the part in 'Glenroe' it was almost like we had known each other for a long time. We fitted in very casually and relaxed into each other's company. We got on with it—he seemed to like me, and I liked him. Particularly in the 'Glenroe' years you would have a great laugh with him, and he was very clever in spotting inadequacies in the script. *Mary McEvoy on actor Mick Lally, who died on the last day of this month.*

What is unusual for me is that my relationship with Mick was through his love of the Irish language. All my conversations for many years with him were through Irish. During my work with him last year on the new Tom Murphy play, *The Last Days of a Reluctant Tyrant*, we didn't speak a word of English together. I could see he used the Irish language, in his connection with folklore and heritage, in his acting. *Abbey Theatre director Fiach Mac Conghail.*

Everything in my life, both professionally and personally, has been intertwined with Mick and his family. Druid would not have existed were it not for Mick, and I find it very hard to take that such an extraordinary life force has gone. *Garry Hynes, joint founder, Druid Theatre Company.*

Swastika laundered

He'd say things like, I mean, he never said actually this, but you'd be eating away and he'd go, 'Ah, you know, that fella Hitler, he had a few good ideas.' The next minute the place would erupt. He'd sit back, and me and my two sisters would argue passionately that we didn't fucking believe it at all. It was fairly explosive. *Bob Geldof on his father, Bob Snr, who died this month at ninety-six.*

HERE & THERE

He has made it into the history books, all the kids know about him. Burke and Wills are up there among the key explorers for Australia. It really is important for us to keep remembering where these people that we, as Australians, regard as heroes actually came from. And in this case it is a Galway man. *Bruce Davis, Australian ambassador to Ireland, on the 150th anniversary of the ill-fated expedition led by Robert O'Hara Burke.*

Cóbh rambler

I've no trouble talking about Cóbh for two-and-a-half hours. I could go on for two-and-a-half weeks, there's so much history here. We have everything from early monasticism to Vikings and Normans, Cromwell, the Famine and beyond. Even locals are amazed just what a history we have. The ships that picked up Alexander Selkirk ... the basis for *Robinson Crusoe,* came via Cóbh. Some twenty-five per cent of all convicts from the UK and Ireland that were shipped to Australia came through here. *Titanic Trail tour guide Michael Martin.*

Jewty done

I came back after two months and wrote a piece on my experiences. Now I am getting hate mail and being targeted. I went into a clothes shop where I live, and the security guard came up to me abusing me. My Facebook page link was posted online in a forum, and I started getting emails telling me to keep my head down from now on. *Cork student Clíona Campbell on working for two months with the Israeli Defence Forces.*

Clare advantage

While I was there I was struck by how suitable it was for a pilot project on the Irish language. Clare Island has a population of 160 people. Its location off the west coast of Ireland is between Mayo and Connemara Gaeltacht areas, yet it is an English-speaking island. I believe it could be an ideal location for a pilot project on learning Irish, where the target could be for Clare Island to become Irish-speaking in the near future. *Frank Feighan TD.*

Direction finder

I say that in Ireland the education and legal systems might be Anglo-Saxon but our culture and way of interacting with people is not. Spaniards complain that northern Europeans are too direct, and northerners complain Spaniards are not direct enough. I spend a lot of time trying to explain one to the other. *Joe Haslam, IE Business School.*

Dislocation

I was planning to go to work in America, and a friend was working in Galway. He said I might as well visit him in Ireland, because all planes stopped in Shannon, so I stopped there. I thought Ireland was part of England at the time, but he told me Ireland was to the left of England. *Dr Ravi Kambamettu, Indian father of Clare Kambamettu, 2010 Rose of Tralee.*

Beefing it up

Americans have hamburger spelling. The quicker, the faster and the easier it goes down the better. There's a lot of enthusiasm but not a lot of formality in their writing. *Marie Louise O'Donnell, Department of Journalism, Dublin City University.*

No go

There are doctors, lawyers, clergymen, politicians, loving parents, talented artists, disabled people, bright, adorable but hopeless children, all camped together for years unending. *Ivo Muma, Mosney Asylum Centre Residents' Committee, Co. Meath.*

HOME AND HOSED

It was like living in the back seat of a Ford Mondeo, being bounced around the place, and it could take you twenty minutes just to change your socks. *Galwayman Ray Campbell on his return from a record-breaking rowing-boat crossing of the Atlantic.*

Index